PROFESSOR BRANESTAWM

Stories

by

Norman Hunter

RED
FOX

Contents

The Professor Invents a Machine
illustrated by W. Heath Robinson 9
Professor Branestawm Having a Brilliant Idea
illustrated by Jill McDonald. 21
Professor Branestawm Up the Pole
illustrated by George Adamson 24
Branestawm's Brain-Teasers I
illustrated by Derek Cousins 39
Press-Button Shopping
illustrated by Derek Cousins 41
How to Push Your Friend Through a
One-centimetre Hole
illustrated by Jill McDonald. 54
Professor Branestawm and the Babies
illustrated by George Adamson 56
Professor Branestawm's Secret Book of Plans
illustrated by Jill McDonald. 65
Professor Branestawm Round the Bend
illustrated by Derek Cousins 68
Everything Handy
illustrated by Jill McDonald. 81

Branestawm's Portable Car Park
illustrated by David Hughes 83
A Finder of Lost Things
illustrated by Jill McDonald 95
The Screaming Clocks
illustrated by W. Heath Robinson 97
Branestawm's Crazy Clock
illustrated by Jill McDonald 109
The Expandable House
illustrated by George Adamson 114
Professor Branestawm's Dictionary Quiz 127
The Professor Stays with Sister Aggie
illustrated by George Adamson 129
Friendly and Unfriendly Needles
illustrated by Jill McDonald 139
The Professor Deals with Inflation
illustrated by Derek Cousins 141
Professor Branestawm and the Secret Agents . . 152
The Unexpected Tale of Professor Flittersnoop
illustrated by George Adamson 157
Professor Flittersnoop and Mrs Branestawm
illustrated by Jill McDonald 170
The Big Zipper
illustrated by Derek Cousins 176
Mrs Flittersnoop Asks for a Rise
illustrated by Derek Cousins 189
To Please Mrs Flittersnoop
illustrated by George Adamson 191
Table-Laying Made Easy
illustrated by Jill McDonald 202
The Pipes of Pandemonium
illustrated by David Hughes 205

Contents

Branestawm's Brain-Teasers II
illustrated by Derek Cousins *218*
The Wild Washing-day
illustrated by Derek Cousins *220*
Professor Branestawm's Incredible Discovery
illustrated by Jill McDonald *232*
The Too-Many Professors
illustrated by W. Heath Robinson *234*
Branestawm's Cross-Figure Puzzle *245*
A Brush with the Artists
illustrated by George Adamson *256*
A Tin that Does as You Tell It
illustrated by Jill McDonald *260*
The Monstrous Memorial
illustrated by Derek Cousins *263*
How to Turn a Pack of Cards into Several Boxes
illustrated by Jill McDonald *275*
The Branestawm Church Service
illustrated by Derek Cousins *278*
A Tower of Match-boxes
illustrated by Jill McDonald *288*
The Professor Borrows a Book
illustrated by W. Heath Robinson *290*

*To the best of readers — all Branestawm
fans throughout the world.*

The Professor
Invents a Machine

Professor Branestawm, like all great men, had simple tastes. He wore simple trousers with two simple legs. His coat was simply fastened with safety pins because the buttons had simply fallen off. His head was simply bald and it simply shone like anything whenever the light caught it.

It was a wonderful head was the Professor's. He had a high forehead to make room for all the pairs of glasses he wore. A pair for reading by. A pair for writing by. A pair for out of doors. A pair for looking at you over the top of and another pair to look for the others when he mislaid them, which was often. For although the Professor was so clever, or perhaps *because* he was so clever, he was very absent-minded. He was so busy thinking of wonderful things like new diseases or new moons that he simply hadn't time to think of ordinary things like old spectacles.

He had very few friends because people found it

so very difficult to talk to him. It was like being at a lecture or in a schoolroom. Every second word he said you couldn't understand and he asked you questions worse than any you'd ever find on an Exam. paper.

But there was one man who was very fond of the Professor. And that was Colonel Dedshott of the Catapult Cavaliers, a very brave gentleman who never missed a train, an enemy, or an opportunity of getting into danger.

'Well, well,' the Colonel was saying to himself in his usual brisk military manner, as he strode along the road towards the house where the Professor lived, 'it's quite a time since I saw Branestawm.' (You can tell how friendly he was with the Professor to talk about him like that, not saying Mr Branestawm or Professor Branestawm or Branestawm Esquire or anything.) 'I am glad he invited me.'

Yes, the Professor had invited him.

'Dear Dedshott,' ran the Professor's note. 'Come and see me tomorrow if you can. I have an invention that will change all our ideas of travel.'

You see the Professor could write quite simple, easy-to-understand letters when he liked. So the Colonel was going to have his ideas of travel changed.

He arrived at the Professor's house, when he got there, to the second. That was his military punctuality.

'The Professor's in his inventory, sir,' said Mrs Flittersnoop, the housekeeper, who opened the door. 'He'll be out directly.'

The words were no sooner out of her mouth than a deafening explosion rent the air and the Professor came out of his inventory. He came out rather more like a cannon-ball than a man welcoming a friend to his house, but he came out, which was the main thing. And most of the inventory came out with him.

When the smoke had cleared away the Professor put his hand to his head, pulled down the pair of glasses that he kept for looking at you over the top of, and looked at the Colonel over the top of them.

'Tut, tut,' he said, 'that was most unfortunate. I had a little too much of the whatever-it-is of the thingummy. I put plenty in to make sure there was enough. I'm afraid I've made rather a mess.'

'Not at all,' said the Colonel. It wasn't his inventory, so why should he mind? 'What do we do next?'

The Professor examined a piece of machinery that had landed on the geranium bed and pushed it into the back garden before replying.

'Happily nothing is damaged,' he said, 'so we can go on from where I left off. This is my new invention.' He patted the machine, which looked something like a cross between a typewriter, an egg-timer, and a conjuring trick.

'Yes,' said the Colonel intelligently, wondering what it was all about.

'Listen,' went on the Professor, 'and I will explain.'

The Colonel sat down on the garden roller and started listening.

'If you travel by coach from this town to the next

it takes two hours,' said the Professor. 'But if you go twice as fast it takes only one hour.'

'Of course,' said the Colonel.

'And if you go twice as fast as that it takes only half an hour.'

'Quite,' said the Colonel.

'And if you go fast enough it takes no time at all, so that you get there the moment you start. Very well ...' The Professor was warming up to his subject and he leaned forward excitedly. 'If you go still faster you will get there in less than no time so that you arrive there before you left here. Do you understand?'

'Perfectly,' said the Colonel, not understanding anything.

'Well then,' went on the Professor, wagging a long thin finger, 'that means that the farther you go, the sooner you will get there, and if you go far enough you will arrive several years ago.'

'Come on,' said the Colonel, getting up with his head going round and round at the very thought of it, 'let's start. I'd like to go back to a party I was at three years ago.'

The Professor, eager to demonstrate his machine, took out a toothpick, a marmalade spoon and a pair of scissors, and soon had the machine wound up and adjusted ready to start.

'Wait a minute,' he cried and ran into the house, coming out a moment later with a small box.

'Bombs,' he explained simply, 'my own invention. Each one will kill an army. We'll take them in case of danger. Are you armed?'

The Colonel nodded and tapped his belt where he always carried his trusty catapult and a bag of bullets.

'Aye,' he said, and they got into the machine together, the Professor falling off on the other side and having to get on again, just as Mrs Flittersnoop came out with a cup of tea for each of them.

'Right away,' called the Professor, who knew all about railways, taking no notice of her.

The Colonel said nothing. He wasn't able to, because as the machine shot off the ground such a gust of wind caught him in the mouth that he could hardly breathe, let alone call out things.

Blue and yellow smoke shot out from every part of the machine. Wheels whizzed. Levers clicked. Little bits of stuff went buzzing up and down and round and round. And far beneath them the landscape rushed by quicker and quicker until at last they could see nothing but a grey haze all round them.

On went the machine, but nothing else happened. On and on they whirled, and nothing happened. And it kept on happening over and over again, till everything was so nothing that neither of them could notice anything.

Presently the Professor thought it was time to stop, so he rang his bell and put the brake on.

Gradually everything began to be something. The grey haze went and the landscape came back and soon they were descending into the middle of a large field.

'Are we there?' asked the Colonel, getting his breath back and using some of it at once.

'We must have passed it,' said the Professor, peering down. 'What's going on down there?'

'Why, it's a battle,' cried the Colonel, loosening his catapult in his belt. 'But it isn't a battle I remember fighting in. Anyway I can't see me there and I should be there if I was, shouldn't I?'

The Professor nodded his head, and then shook it to show that he understood.

'You weren't there,' he said, 'we're in Squiglatania, a foreign country. I know this battle. It happened two years ago. There was a revolution, but the King's troops beat the revolutionists. Those are the King's troops, the red ones.'

'Let's join in,' cried the Colonel, and at once he began firing off bullets from his catapult, while the Professor opened his box and rained his deadly bombs on the scene below, as the machine dropped slowly downwards.

Gock, boom, smack, pop, boom. Twack, boom, clack, plop, boom, went the bombs and the catapult bullets, and by the time the machine touched the ground there was hardly a soldier or a revolutionist left.

'Hurray,' yelled the Colonel, jumping out and rushing about, followed by the Professor.

'Hurray,' yelled a little band of revolutionists, who had been hiding behind some rocks. 'We've won, thanks to you.'

And before the Professor and the Colonel knew where they were, the revolutionists carried them off to the Palace and sat them on the King's throne, which happily was wide enough for both of them, as the King had been a very fat man.

AND SAT THEM
ON THE KING'S
THRONE. —

'Hail, our Presidents!' they shouted.

And bands played, fireworks went off, people danced and ate more than was good for them, to celebrate the victory.

'This is all wrong, you know,' said the Professor, 'it was the King's troops who won really. We've done something nasty to history, I'm afraid. I had no idea we should alter the battle like that.'

'Never mind,' said the Colonel, who rather fancied himself as a President. 'Let's do some ruling.'

But whether it was that the Professor, although he knew so much about everything, didn't know enough about ruling; or whether it was that the Colonel, not being used to such high command, gave himself airs rather too much; or whether it was that the Revolutionist people, who didn't like being governed by one King, found it wasn't any more fun being governed by two Presidents, things didn't go at all well.

First there was trouble about who should wear the crown. It was too small for the Professor's brainy head, and too big for the Colonel's bullet head.

Then the Colonel wanted to review the troops and there weren't any troops. They'd all been blown to bits with the Professor's bombs or catapulted with the Colonel's catapult, so he had to play with toy soldiers from the Palace Nursery. And of course no real live Colonel cares much about that sort of thing.

HAD TO PLAY WITH
TOY SOLDIERS.

Then the Professor wanted to go on inventing things, and there wasn't an inventory at the Palace and nobody knew how to make one, so he had to put up with the chicken-house at the end of the grounds. But by the time he had got his wonderful machine inside it there wasn't any more room, either for the Professor or for the chickens.

'I'm tired of this life,' said the Colonel one day. 'Let's do something else.'

'What can we do?' said the Professor. 'If we get on the machine we shall only go back earlier and earlier and have to wait longer and longer.'

Just then the Chief Revoluter came in, sword in one hand and a bunch of keys in the other.

THE CHIEF
REVOLUTER

17

'We've decided not to have any Presidents,' he said. 'You're dethroned. Your services are no longer required, take a week's notice.'

'Don't take any notice,' whispered the Colonel, who didn't see why they should be spoken to like that.

'We refuse,' said the Professor, looking at the Chief Revoluter through all his pairs of glasses at once, and wondering why he looked so dim and hazy and funny-shaped. 'Go away, there's something wrong with you. You must have been sleeping with your eyes open, or else you washed your face the wrong way round. You're all out of shape. Go away at once, we're busy.' And he started adding up threes by the dozen on his shirt-cuff to look as if he had a lot to do.

'Stay,' cried the Chief Revoluter, waving his keys by mistake and quickly changing hands and waving his sword instead, 'get off the throne or be thrown off.'

'Ha, ha!' laughed the Colonel, who always saw a joke if it was an easy one.

'Ho, ho!' cried the Chief Revoluter, who was now very much annoyed.

'Hum, hum,' said the Professor, 'four three's are twelve, five three's are fifteen, six three's are . . . I do wish you'd go away and leave me to my accounts.'

'Guards!' cried the Chief Revoluter, banging his keys with his sword to make a jangling noise like an alarm.

'Yes?' asked the guards coming in.

'To the Dungeons with them,' cried the Chief Revoluter.

'Gr-r-r-r-r,' growled the guards, guessing that they were expected to be fierce. 'To the Dungeons,' and drawing their swords they rushed at the Colonel and the Professor, who got up and jumped out of the window.

'After them,' yelled the Chief Revoluter, standing aside to let the guards chase them.

They dashed across the croquet lawn, where a lot of the guards who didn't understand croquet caught their feet in the hoops and fell over, thus delaying the chase.

Through the grounds raced the Professor and the Colonel, down to the chicken-house where the machine was kept.

'We must get away,' panted the Professor, 'never mind where or when to.'

They clambered on the machine, and the Professor pulled some levers.

Zoom, crash, bang! A terrific explosion rent the air. The chicken-house vanished. So did the Palace of Squiglatania. So did everything. And the next minute the Colonel and the Professor were rolling on the Professor's lawn, and Mrs Flittersnoop was handing them a cup of tea each.

The day they first started had come round again and, of course, as they were on the Professor's lawn when they started, they had to be there again.

'One or two lumps?' asked Mrs Flittersnoop, meaning sugar.

'One on the back of my head and two on my knees,' answered the Professor, meaning bruises from his fall.

So they were all right again. The Colonel could go on commanding the Catapult Cavaliers, the Professor could go on inventing. But the people who write the history books had an awful time clearing up the tangle they'd made of Squiglatanian history by winning a battle for the side that really lost it.

From *The Incredible Adventures of Professor Branestawm*

Professor Branestawm Having a Brilliant Idea

This is a working model of the Professor showing how he acts when he has been hit with one of his famous and ingeniously disastrous ideas.

The first thing to do is to cut out the pieces of cardboard for the Professor's body, arms and legs. Figure 1 shows how to do this, with the measurements. You can make the figure bigger but don't make it much smaller because a small figure is difficult to work. Paint the pieces on both sides.

Make holes in the pieces as shown in the diagram.

Now join the arms and legs to the body. This must be done so that they will move freely. Use the lower of the two holes at the top of the arms and legs as shown in Figure 2. If Dad has a workshop you could get him to fix the pieces together with rivets so that they work easily. Otherwise you can fix them together with the kind of paper fasteners that push through and bend over, but see that the holes are

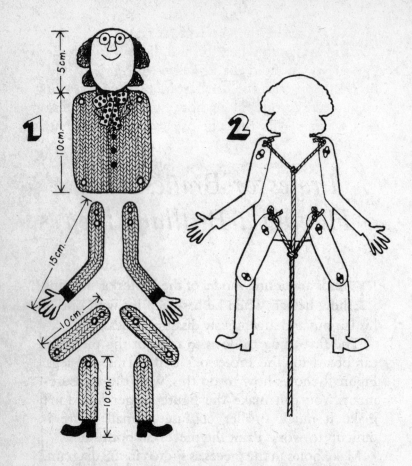

large enough for the pieces to move freely and don't fasten them together at all tightly.

Now tie a piece of thick thread or thin string to the extra holes in the arms so that you have a loop of string hanging across the back of the figure. Do the same with the legs. Tie one end of a long piece of string round the centre of the loop between the arms. Carry the string down and tie it round the loop of string between the two legs. Arms and legs should be hanging down when this is done. See Figure 2.

Now if you hold the Professor with one hand by his head and with the other you pull the long string up and down you will see how excited the Professor gets when he has thought of a world-shaking new invention.

From *Professor Branestawm's Do-It-Yourself Handbook*

Why does Professor Branestawm sleep with his five pairs of spectacles on? *So that he can see what he is dreaming about.*

Professor Branestawm
Up the Pole

Professor Branestawm had a new next-door neighbour, Commander Hardaport (Retired), a ferociously enthusiastic, yachting sort of Commander. He wore a white-topped yachting cap all day, and sometimes all night if he forgot to take it off. And in his garden he had a flagstaff on which he flew a most elegant flag.

He got up every morning at sunrise to hoist the flag up the pole and was always most particular to lower it again at sunset, because leaving flags out all night is highly irregular and very bad manners. It was awkward for Commander Hardaport sometimes in the winter, when he went to tea with friends, because, right in the middle of tea and intensive talk about spinnakers and yardarms, sunset would come on. Then he had to dash home to lower his flag and by the time he got back his friends had finished the cakes (but no, of course, the yachting conversation, which, unlike flags, can quite properly go flying on all night).

'Flagstaff's looking a bit dirty,' he said to himself one morning. 'Most un-white flagstaff I've ever seen. This won't do at all. I'll have to get to action stations. But what course to set? Re-paint it? Then what? The flagstaff will get dirty again. His naval mind revolved rapidly both forward and astern. 'What I need', he said, 'is some flagstaff paint that won't get dirty. I know – I'll get Professor Branestawm to invent some. Right. Ahoy there, Professor Branestawm!' he shouted over the fence.

Mrs Flittersnoop, the Professor's housekeeper, was in the middle of hanging out the washing. 'I'm afraid Professor Branestawm is out,' she said. She wasn't afraid of it really, but was actually glad because it gave her a chance to tidy the place up a bit. 'Can I give him a message when he comes back?'

'Thank you, but this is complicated,' said the Commander. 'I'd better send him a signal. Don't want to get things confused.' And he stumped into his house, and went into a tiny little room with a round porthole window and walls smothered in telescopes and charts and binnacles and bollards and hung about with warps and halliards.

'Dear Professor Branestawm,' he wrote, and was just going to ask the Professor to invent a never-get-dirty paint when an idea struck him amidships. After all, inventing a paint was rather a silly job for an inventing professor. The paint shop could do that. He had a much more important thing for Professor

Branestawm to do.

He finished the letter, put it in an envelope, addressed it 'To Professor Branestawm. Message from the flagstaff', which was another of his seagoing jokes, and handed it over to Mrs Flittersnoop.

Then he wrote another letter to the paint shop saying, 'Will you please supply me with some white paint for my flagstaff. And I want paint that will never get dirty.' Then his pen, which had gone a bit scratchy, ran out of ink and he had to sign the note 'Hector Hardaport (Retired)' in pencil. But he used blue pencil to make it look as nautical as possible.

'Ah,' said Professor Branestawm, when he read the Commander's letter. 'A most interesting and unusual request.' He looked at the letter through each of his five pairs of spectacles and then through several pairs at once. 'The Commander wishes me to invent a flagstaff-painting machine,' he said.

'Well, I never, sir,' said Mrs Flittersnoop. 'These naval gentlemen have some very strange ideas at times. Or perhaps I should say rum ideas.' These seafaring jokes were catching.

Then the Professor went into his inventory to invent the flagstaff-painting machine.

'I could, of course, ah, do it by first inventing a gatepost-painting machine and then re-inventing it much taller,' he said to himself. 'Or I might just invent a painting machine with a special adjustment for height and width. But then again I could invent a machine through which one pushed the, um, ah, flagstaff to paint it, but that might be awkward as the Commander would possibly not want to take the flagstaff down.'

After inventing like this for a while, the Professor finally got down to the flagstaff-painting machine, which was a device that you rode rather like a bicycle and it climbed up the flagstaff while you did the painting.

Then he set off for the Great Pagwell High Street, thinking he might meet the Commander cruising about among the shops. And he hadn't got far when he met the Commander, rolling nautically down the High Street in a way that made you feel there was a heavy swell running, and that the High Street was taking it green over the bows. He was smoking a pipe that sent out such a smoke screen that the Professor wouldn't have seen him only he happened to be looking the other way. That caused him to run into the Commander, who bellowed, 'Hard astern both!', shook the Professor by the hand, and said, 'Fancy meeting you on a collision course, Professor! How's the machine coming on?'

'I, er, am glad to say it is all ready, Commander,' said the Professor. 'Where would you like it delivered?'

'On to the jolly old flagstaff!" cried the Commander, laughing like a ship's ventilator with the wind. 'I will go and arrange for you to carry out the operation.'

He gave the Professor a hearty seafaring clap on the back which shook all his spectacles off and, before the Professor had time to say anything, he was off in a cloud of heavy smoke.

The next day Professor Branestawm, accompanied by

his flagstaff-painting machine, came over the fence. He was dressed in some painter's overalls, lent to him by Mrs Flittersnoop's sister Aggie's cousin Bert. They were on the big side and Mrs Flittersnoop had fixed them up with plenty of safety pins.

He looked up at the flagstaff, which appeared to be at least two miles high. Then he clamped the painting machine round the bottom of the flagstaff and got into the saddle.

'Here's the paint,' said the Commander, giving him a tin with a handle on it. 'And a brush.'

'Er, ah, thank you,' said the Professor. He put the tin of paint into the paint-holder on the machine and put the brush in his mouth so as to have both hands free to start the machine, which was necessary as the machine had innumerable buttons and levers.

He pulled two levers and twiddled a wheel. With a series of grunts, squeaks and rattles the machine began very slowly to climb the flagstaff and the Professor began to paint.

Squeak, rattle, zimzim, popetty clank, went the machine. *Slip, slop, slosh*, went the Professor with the paint brush.

'Avast there!' shouted the Commander. 'What are you starting at the bottom for?'

'Because one must always start at the bottom,' said the Professor. All the best copybooks say so. You could not have risen to become a Commander by starting at the top as an Admiral. There is also the ratio of height tolerance to speed to be considered. If, for instance,' he waved both hands and fell off the seat of the machine, 'if, for instance, you get into a motor car and start driving at a hundred miles an hour right away you are liable to, um, ah, have an accident because you have not had time to accustom yourself to the speed.'

'Hrmmph. Quite,' said a voice from behind. It was the Professor's old friend, Colonel Dedshott of the Catapult Cavaliers, who had just arrived on his horse, which was rather given to starting off at full speed if it could.

'So,' said the Professor, climbing back on the seat of the painting machine, 'you start slowly and gradually build up the speed, and so become used to the fast movement by degrees.'

He was nine inches up the flagstaff when Mrs Flittersnoop from next door called out, 'Telephone, sir,' and the Professor had to go rushing in to answer the telephone. But it was only the Vicar to ask how the flagstaff-painting was going.

Next the Professor was two feet nine inches up the flagstaff when Mrs Flittersnoop called out that lemonade and sponge cakes were ready. So they all knocked off for a lemonade-break, which is the same as a coffee-break but sometimes takes longer. It certainly did this time because no sooner had Commander Hardaport finished a stirring yarn about naval escapades than Colonel Dedshott, not be outdone by a mere sailor, opened fire with an intrepid story about fighting against dreadful odds in the desert. And that reminded the Professor of the time he invented an outrageous cactus that put umbrellas up if you watered it.

So, after all that, the lemonade-break lasted until

lunch-time. Mrs Flittersnoop said she had just made one of her special steak and kidney puddings, and had new potatoes and peas to go with it, and a frightfully fancy trifle to follow it. Neither the military nor the naval part of the party could resist that, and even the Professor actually ate lunch because his mind wasn't entirely on the flagstaff-painting project.

And they all ate so much they went to sleep afterwards and woke up only just in time for tea. Then the Vicar called to see how they were getting on and the Headmaster of Pagwell College came round with advice about flagstaffs, which he felt competent to give as he had once had to climb the college flagstaff to get down his mortar-board hat, which an energetic pupil had put up there for a joke.

By the time they had got through all these serious matters it was too dark to do any painting, so the company dismissed until next day.

Next day it rained, and apart from a suggestion from the Professor that they should bring the flagstaff indoors to paint it, which was ruled out as nobody had a room long enough, the entire day was wasted.

But at last there came a day when it was fine, and the Commander and the Colonel had run out of thrilling stories, and Mrs Flittersnoop had gone to the supermarket and couldn't serve lemonade and sponge cakes, and the Vicar and the Headmaster were too busy to call, and flagstaff painting could therefore begin in earnest.

Slap, slosh, slap, the Professor painted away at the flagstaff. *Creak, creak, rattle, squeak*, the machine

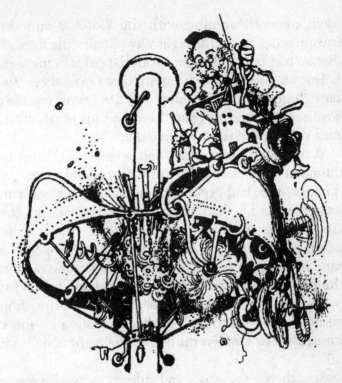

gradually crawled up the staff as he painted. People stopped outside to offer useful advice and make encouraging noises. Up and up went the Professor until at last he was right at the top and the whole flagstaff was gleaming white. Certain portions of the Colonel and the Commander were also gleaming white where the Professor had spilt a drop or two of paint now and again.

But oh good gracious! Of course the Professor ought to have realized that the higher up he painted the flagstaff the more he wouldn't be able to get down because of the wet paint. But he had been so taken up with arguing with the Colonel and the Commander about the right way to paint the flagstaff that he had never thought about the paint being wet.

But oh good gracious ninety times over, there was something else! Something the Professor couldn't have remembered because he didn't know about it. And neither did the Commander.

When the Commander had written the letter to the paint shop asking for paint that would never get dirty, his pen had gone scratchy at the end and run out of ink and he had had to sign it in pencil. But the Commander hadn't noticed that the running-out pen had written the word 'dirty' so that it looked like 'dry' because some of the letters hadn't come out. So the Commander's letter had asked the paint shop for paint that would never get dry. And the paint shop people hadn't worried. They had just put a bit more linseed oil, or whatever it is, into the paint and sent it off.

So there it was, and there was Professor Branestawm, stuck on top of a lovely, clean, newly painted, sixty-foot flagstaff which would never dry to let him come down.

Colonel Dedshott and the Commander had no idea things were as awful as they really were. But Professor Branestawm had. He had just remembered to read the instructions on the tin of paint now the job was finished, because that is when people usually read instructions if they ever do.

'Dedshott!' he called through his portable radio, that fortunately he had taken up with him in case he wanted to listen to any learned talks while he painted. And fortunately again, it was a radio for broadcasting from as well as listening to. 'Dedshott!' he said. 'I have just seen printed on this tin of paint that it will never get dry. I am stuck up here for ever. Get help!'

The Colonel and the Commander couldn't hear him. They hadn't got any radio receivers. But the Professor's radio went right into the Pagwell Broadcasting Company's programme. Mrs Flittersnoop, listening in the kitchen to Willie Wibblesome's half-hour, heard the Professor's call for help right in the middle of a song about someone loving someone for three times over.

'Lawks a mussy me!' she cried. 'If that isn't the Professor calling for help.' She dashed out into the garden and shouted to Commander Hardaport, 'It's the Professor, sir! Broadcasting on the wireless, sir! Asking for Colonel Dedshott to help, sir. Something about the paint never drying, he said.'

Commander Hardaport dashed into his house and came out again with a loud-hailer of the kind that ships use to argue with one another at sea.

Then there started a most unlikely, complicated, long distance conversation, with the Commander and Colonel Dedshott loud-hailing questions up to the Professor, and the Professor answering them through Mrs Flittersnoop's kitchen radio. And Mrs Flittersnoop running backwards and forwards with messages.

'By Jove, what!' cried the Colonel,. his head spinning round and round faster than it did when he was listening to one of the Professor's complicated explanations. 'How are we to get him down, Commander? No equipment for climbing wet flagstaffs. Never found an enemy up a flagstaff yet. You get the Navy, sir. They're used to climbing masts and things. They'll have the Professor down in no time, by gad!'

'Nothing of the kind!' protested Commander Hardaport. 'Not even the Navy can climb masts covered in wet paint. Ridiculous, sir. Fetch the Fire Brigade!'

'Right! Good idea!' shouted the Colonel.

He burst off and almost immediately Commander Hardaport was hit with a clever idea. If the Navy couldn't climb wet flagstaffs they *could* erect dry flagstaffs. Yes, yes, indeed. And he, Commander Hardaport, would get them to erect one next to his, so that they could get the Professor down.

'Can't hold on much longer!' came an anguished message from the Professor, via Mrs Flittersnoop.

'Hold on just a bit,' shouted the Commander through his loud-hailer. He dashed into the Professor's house and got Mrs Flittersnoop to help him out with an armchair. Then tying this to a rope with many nautical knots, he threw the rope up to the Professor, so that he didn't have to go on sitting in the painting machine, which was hard and irksome for sitting in for ever.

After that things happened fast and thick.

The Professor hauled up the armchair by the rope and fixed it on top of the flagstaff, and sent the rope down for a little table and some books to read. Then he got the Commander to hoist up some of his

inventing tools and before long he was sitting up on the flagstaff, sixty feet above everything, inventing like mad.

'Now if I could, ah, um, invent a way of getting down from here . . .' he said. But that was the one thing he couldn't do.

Meantime the Fire Brigade arrived and so did the Navy, or at least some of it. The flagstaff-erecting began in earnest but didn't get on very fast because the firemen and their ladder kept getting tangled up with the sailors and their flagstaff.

'Avast there!' shouted the Commander. 'Lower away, haul up a bit! Keep that ladder away there!'

And the Fire Brigade Chief was shouting to the firemen, and Colonel Dedshott was shouting to the Professor through the loud-hailer. And the Professor was shouting back to the Colonel via Mrs Flittersnoop and the kitchen radio. And the road was thicker with sightseers then if it had been Lord Mayor's Show day.

Three times the Navy got their flagstaff up at the same time as the Fire Brigade got their ladder up. Firemen ran up the ladder and slid down the flagstaff, while sailors swarmed up the flagstaff and ran down the ladder. The Professor invented several kinds of paint that would dry as soon as you put them on, and one that came out in little steps so that you could go down them like a staircase.

But the ladder and flagstaff weren't near enough for the Professor to come down.

Colonel Dedshott began to see visions of himself going up the spare flagstaff on horseback to have tea with the Professor. Mrs Flittersnoop started wondering how she was going to haul meals up a flagstaff. The Mayor's wife, who was used to doing Meals-on-Wheels, offered to try her hand at meals-on-ropes. The Colonel and the Commander sent up a camp bed and some of Mrs Flittersnoop's second-best blankets.

Then along came the Pagwell Electricity Department with one of those tall tower arrangements they use for putting new lamps in the lamp-posts.

'Soon have you down from there, now, sir,' said the chief electricity man, winding the tower up alongside the Professor.

But by now Professor Branestawm was so comfortable on top of the flagstaff and found it so peaceful with nobody to disturb his inventing and no telephone calls and no bills able to reach him, that he wanted to stay up there.

The electricity chief, always willing to help, rigged up a nice street lamp so that the Professor could see after dark.

'But he can't stay up there for ever!' said Dr Mumpzanmeazle.

'Hrmmph!' said Colonel Dedshott.

'Ridiculous!' snorted Commander Hardaport (Retired).

'Oh dearie, dearie me!' wailed Mrs Flittersnoop.

'I fear this is most, er, most, er, er,' said the Vicar.

And goodness knows what would have been the end of it all, but just then it came on to rain. It pelted. It poured. The looking-on crowds went home. The Fire Brigade went off in a hurry reckoning the rain could put out any fires that happened, and the Navy left because it was sunset and they had to haul their flags down.

But fortunately the electricity man and his tower stayed on because providing light, even in the rain, was his job. And the Professor, who wouldn't have come down to save getting himself wet because he could have had an umbrella slung up to him, was absolutely terrified that his books and inventing tools would be spoiled.

So he crawled gingerly on to the electric light tower and was lowered gently to the ground amid three cheers, one from Colonel Dedshott, one from

Commander Hardaport and a very faint but none the less enthusiastic one from Mrs Flittersnoop.

But the non-drying paint on the flagstaff collected all the dirt it could find, and it looked more of an un-nautical mess than ever. And worst of all the Commander couldn't hoist his flag up it or the flag would have got covered in paint, which would have been frightful.

But everything ended up very nicely after all. The Commander took down the dirty flagstaff and instead Professor Branestawm invented a special automatic, self-acting flagstaff that hoisted the flag all by itself at sunrise and lowered it again at sunset. So the Commander didn't have to get up at the crack of dawn any more, and neither did he have to come dashing back from enjoyable parties to haul the flag down.

And the Branestawm automatic flagstaff not only hoisted the flag every day at sunrise, including Sundays and holidays, but it also played 'God Save the Queen' as it did so. It played it fairly quietly, of course, so as not to disturb the neighbours, which was important, particularly as Professor Branestawm was one of the neighbours.

But Commander Hardaport (Retired) still felt he ought to wake up at sunrise anyway, so as to stand up and salute while the flag went up and the music went off.

There's no satisfying some people.

From *Professor Branestawm Up the Pole*

Branestawm's
Brain-Teasers I

Why is a river like a spoon used for eating custard?
Because it goes from sauce to mouth.

Why are soldiers tired in April?
Because they've just had a thirty-one day March.

How does a champion athlete stop music playing?
By breaking records.

What is the most dishonest animal in the zoo?
The cheetah.

How do you hire a table?
Put a book under each leg.

What can go up a chimney down, but can't go down
a chimney up?
An umbrella

Where do you find things going cheap?
In the Canary Islands.

What does a bus conductor say to children whose
parents get on the bus when it is full?
Pass father down the bus, please.

From *Professor Branestawm's Compendium*

Press-Button
Shopping

Professor Branestawm was furious. He didn't often get furious, but this time he was. He clashed his spectacles, he gnashed his teeth, he stamped about.

'I, er, um, ah, pah!' he snorted.

It was all the fault of the Great Pagwell Bank. Not that they'd made any difficulties about letting him have money. Absolutely on the contrary. They'd made it too easy for everyone to get money, even when the bank was shut.

Yes, most dire and dreadful thing, the bank had actually invented a money-paying-out machine. You just pressed buttons and the money you wanted came out, as long as you first put in a special card. Highly ingenious. Oh dear, yes, but highly un-what's-its-name as far as Professor Branestawm was concerned. How dare banks go inventing machines? How absolutely dare they trespass on the Professor's preserves. He didn't trespass on theirs, did he? He didn't accept money deposits and pay interest on them. He didn't issue cheque books and stand behind bars weighing up money. No wonder he was furious when he saw the machine outside the Pagwell Bank.

'Disgraceful!' he cried to Mrs Flittersnoop when he got home. 'Banks have no right to go inventing machines. That is my job as a Professor of, er, thingummy. Oh, I know you invented an invention once, Mrs Flittersnoop,' he added, 'but that was just an idea for not going up and down stairs so often. It wasn't a *machine*. And anyway,' he smiled at Mrs Flittersnoop and his spectacles went crooked, 'you are one of the family so to speak, so that doesn't count.'

Mrs Flittersnoop wasn't absolutely sure she wanted to be one of the Professor's family, but she just said, 'Yes, indeed, I'm sure, sir,' and took away a cup of coffee just in time for the Professor not to bring his fist down on it. But he brought his fist down on a jam tart instead and stamped off to the bank again with it still sticking to him.

'It won't, um, ah, do, you know,' said the Professor to the bank manager. 'Banks can't go inventing machines. And suppose it goes wrong? Machines do, you know.'

'It has,' groaned the bank manager. 'Three times this morning and twice yesterday. Some of my customers were rather offended at what the machine said to them.'

'You must stop it at once and I will invent a money

machine for you, if you must have one,' said the Professor, scraping the jam tart off into the bank manager's in-tray. He tipped it into the waste-paper basket, where it lay earning no interest whatsoever.

'No, no, my dear Professor,' said the bank manager, 'I think our machine is quite adequate. No doubt it will settle down. It's just that people aren't used to using it and they make mistakes.'

'It is you who made the mistake, inventing the machine in the first place,' snorted the Professor. 'I shall show you I am not a man to be trifled with. I shall invent a rival machine for shoppers which will put yours in the shade,' and he stamped out, leaving the bank manager in such a dither he had to go and count a lot of other people's money to make himself feel better.

Mr Pryce-Rize of the Pagwell Supermarket was delighted when the Professor explained his idea for a shopping machine.

'Terrific, my dear Professor!' he cried, knocking two pence off a jar of raspberry jam and knocking five jars of rather vicious marmalade off a shelf in his excitement. 'It will mean people can shop after we are closed. It will save queues at the pay desks. It will be better than your floating supermarket because we shall not have the River Pag Controllers to worry us.'*

They shook hands and the Professor went home without taking advantage of any of the breath-taking-money-saving-limited-time offers that leered at him on the way out.

*see *Professor Branestawm Round the Bend*

'Mrs Flittersnoop,' he called, as he came in at the kitchen door because he'd forgotten his front door key.

'Oh!' exclaimed Mrs Flittersnoop. 'You did startle me, I'm sure, sir.' She'd have dropped a bowl of cake mixture if she'd been holding one, but thank goodness she wasn't, as Mrs Flittersnoop's cake mixture was very tenacious and would have been difficult to detach from the floor.

'I beg your pardon,' said the Professor, putting his hat on the stove, but Mrs Flittersnoop snatched it up again before it could get over-cooked. 'I am going to invent a machine for people to do their shopping, so that they can shop when the shop is shut and don't have to wait in queues to pay, which they couldn't do if the shop was shut, you follow me?'

'Yes, indeed, I'm sure, sir,' said Mrs Flittersnoop, wiping her hands on her apron and making up her mind this was going to be another of those days.

'Come into the inventory,' said the Professor. 'I shall need your advice as to the kind of, er, groceries and other things shoppers wish to purchase.'

Then began a piece of inventing such as Mrs Flittersnoop had never known before and certainly hoped to escape knowing again.

The Professor asked questions, made notes, constructed models, altered and revised them, took them to bits, rebuilt them, asked more questions, didn't listen to the answers, couldn't find the long-nosed pliers and lost his spectacles among the files.

After inventing like this for some time, Mrs Flittersnoop gave up helping and retired to make cups of tea. Then Colonel Dedshott arrived, just in time to have his head made to go round and round as the Professor explained his invention.

'It is an idea I got from some absurd machine they have at the bank,' said the Professor. 'You just press buttons and it gives you money.'

'By Jove! Jolly good, what!' said the Colonel, who wouldn't have minded pressing a lot of buttons for money as he was sometimes pressed for it a bit himself.

'Banks, in my opinion,' went on the Professor, 'should confine themselves to, ah, er, to, that is to say they shouldn't invent machines. I told the bank manager so, and I am now inventing a machine that will show the bank where it, um, ah, gets off.'

The Colonel, who knew where to get off his horse at the bank, didn't quite see why the bank needed showing where to get off, as it was already there. But he knew better than to say so.

'This system of pressing buttons to obtain articles', went on the Professor, 'is capable of much interesting and intricate development. I am arranging a dial-your-grocer system which is more efficient than "pick and pay" or "pay as you earn" or "serve yourself" or any of the other methods now in, er, vogue.'

'Ha, my word, yes,' said the Colonel, sitting down on a box while his head did unmilitary about-turns and started going round anti-clockwise.

'It's very simple,' said the Professor, pointing to no end of highly complicated pieces of machinery. 'When this is erected outside the supermarket, all a customer has to do is spell out what he wants and the machine will deliver it. No hunting on the shelves for things the supermarket people have, um, ah, moved to a different place. No waiting in queues to pay for the goods. And', the Professor wagged a finger, 'you can buy things even when the shop is shut.'

'Wonderful, by Jove!' grunted the Colonel, who was never very keen on buying things in shops even when they were open, as the lady assistants scared him a bit.

Getting the Professor's shopping machine assembled outside the Pagwell Supermarket was an operation slightly less dangerous than the battle of Agincourt, took rather less time than a trip to the moon, and didn't involve quite so many people as the building of the pyramids. But it ran all these notable events a close second.

First of all the machine was so large it had to be brought to the supermarket in bits. Then people had to stand guard over the bits in case they were stolen or damaged, while more bits were brought along. This caused a nice traffic jam in the High Street while the stuff was unloaded and a rather over-enthusiastic traffic warden gave a ticket to the Chief Policeman for stopping his car on quadruple yellow lines, which mean not only that you mustn't stop there, but that you have no right to be in a car at all.

Then bits of the supermarket had to be pulled out to make room for the machine. Notices were put up inside the supermarket apologizing for any incon-venience caused, but whether the customers accepted the apologies nobody knows.

Then the work of erecting the machine went on all night with changes and bangs and shouts of 'A bit more to you, Les,' and 'Hold 'er up there, Jim,' and 'Where's me flowering spanner?' and other industrial talk.

People complained that they couldn't sleep, but the Professor pointed out that the noise was no more than that of a jumbo jet passing overhead, which happened several times a day and night, usually when you were on the telephone or had just got to sleep.

At last the great Branestawm Shopping Machine was fully installed and ready for action. The Mayor was invited to dial the first order, but said he'd rather not as he had a grocery shop of his own which he couldn't leave unattended. So Mrs Flittersnoop was chosen as representative of a typical shopper, which she didn't think she was and very likely wasn't, to sort of launch the machine.

The Professor stood by with explanations which were hardly needed as the machine did all the explaining necessary itself. There was a notice on it which said 'Dial the name of the article required on the alphabetical keys. Then dial the number or quantity required on the numbered keys and those marked with weights and measures. When you have completed your order press the key marked Total. The amount due will appear in the window at the top of the machine and a drawer will open. Place the money in the drawer, close it and pull the lever. Your order will then be delivered ready for you to take away.'

'It all seems very nice, I'm sure, sir,' said Mrs

Flittersnoop nervously. She approached the machine with her shopping list in one hand and the first finger of the other pointing out ready for key-pressing.

The assembled crowd of housewives, young girls and their boyfriends, spare policemen and Mrs Pryce-Rize of the Pagwell Supermarket all applauded, except for the policemen, who weren't sure whether applauding was legal while on duty.

Mrs Flittersnoop pressed keys, spelling out 'PLUM JAM', and pressed the 1 key. Then she spelt out 'GRANULATED SUGAR KILOS ½' followed by 'TEA BISCUITS GRAMS 250' and 'LEMONADE BOTTLES SMALL 6'. She pressed the Total button and the amount appeared in the window. She put the exact money in the drawer that had opened, closed the drawer and pulled the lever.

There were whirrings, clicks and buzzes. Things seemed to be going ground rapidly and slowly both at once. Then there was an extra loud clang, a door opened and out slid a trolley basket with Mrs Flittersnoop's order neatly stacked in it. On the trolley there was another notice which said 'When you have unloaded the trolley bring it back and place it in the empty compartment at the left of the machine.' The notice then added the warning: 'Trolleys not returned within two hours will emit a high-pitched scream as a safeguard against theft.'

'Well, I never!' exclaimed Mrs Flittersnoop, and there was a rush for the machine by the other shoppers who wanted to try it themselves.

'Most satisfactory, excellent, my dear Professor,' said

Mr Pryce-Rize. 'I'm getting customers from other shops because people enjoy playing with the machine, and it saves my staff a lot of work.'

But, of course, a Branestawm invention wasn't going to let people have things all their own way, never mind how many lettered and numbered keys they pressed.

On the second day after it was installed a lady who wanted a sponge cake for tea dialled 'SPONGE 1' and got a large bath sponge.

Two days later another shopper wanting a nice pudding dialled 'CHOCOLATE MOUSSE,' but left out one 's' and got a little brown, sweet mouse. And another lady got a toy dog instead of the Chinese food she wanted when she dialled 'CHOW CHOW.'

Some of the shoppers weren't so hot at spelling, but the machine did its worst to oblige.

Someone who wanted lettuce got a lot of envelopes with saucy messages in them. Another shopper who wanted minced beef to make shepherd's pie got a roll of peppermints, while a request for steak produced a long thick wooden stick.

Miss Frenzie of the Pagwell Publishing Company, who was immersed in another of her frantic recipe books, came hurtling along and tried to get a packet of cornflour, but the machine misunderstood her and gave her a little blue plastic daisy.

Mrs Trumpington-Smawl arrived with a shopping list three yards long and ordered so many high-class and expensive groceries the machine ran out of trolleys and began firing parcels at her.

She was so annoyed at this that she dialled a ticking off complaint on the machine, to which the machine replied with an extremely rude word in the totalling window.

'Disgraceful!' snorted Mrs Trumpington-Smawl. She dialled a severe reply and got a very insulting answer.

Just then the Vicar came up, listened carefully to what Mrs Trumpington-Smawl had to say, read what the machine had said to her and got so confused that in trying to dial 'INSTANT COFFEE' he got mixed up and the machine gave him incense and a packet of toffee.

The Vicar dialled 'BEHAVE YOURSELF!' and the machine answered 'GET LOST' and delivered an out-of-date map to help him.

The Vicar lost his cool and delivered a kick at the machine, which retaliated with a 2p-off-packet of biscuits well smashed up.

'Disgraceful!' cried the Vicar, attacking the machine with his umbrella.

The machine let fly with cut-price bananas.

Colonel Dedshott arrived and tried to help tame the machine, but it put out complicated military orders and gave him a jar of military pickle.

The Colonel and the Vicar were joined by Commander Hardaport (Retired) and between them they got the machine in such a tiz it started sending out trolley loads of unwanted groceries of all kinds into the High Street traffic.

Then Mr Pryce-Rize got on the telephone to the Professor.

'Come at once, Professor,' he begged. 'Your machine has gone berserk. The High Street is in turmoil.'

Professor Branestawm arrived on the scene just in time to be given half a hundredweight of breakfast cereal. Mr Pryce-Rize came panting up, waving his arms.

'I, um, ah, think it needs some slight adjustment,' said the Professor. He twiddled some wheels on the machine which promptly called him an impolite name and gave him two empty lemonade bottles and a tin of drain un-stopper.

'No, no, no, no!' cried Mr Pryce-Rize. 'Don't adjust it! Stop it! I don't want it.'

'But I thought it had been such an, um, ah, success,' said the Professor, dodging a jar of peanut butter.

'Yes, yes, but too successful,' wailed Mr Pryce-Rize. 'People like the machine so much they're forming longer queues at the machine than they did in the shop. My cashiers have nothing to do. They're knitting woolly jumpers and learning to play the bassoon, in my time. Get rid of the thing, *please*, Professor.'

'Oh, ah, well,' said the Professor. But by this time the Colonel, the Vicar, Commander Hardaport and a few spare policemen had at last managed to get the better of the machine and it was in bits across the High Street.

'Well I think it's a pity, sir,' said Mrs Flittersnoop to the Professor later. 'It did save having to hunt for the things you want and these supermarkets do keep shifting things about, I'm sure, sir.'

So that was the end of the Professor's wonderful shopping machine. Mr Pryce-Rize got his cashiers off their bassoons and knitted jumpers and Professor Branestawm took his machine to pieces and made it into typewriters for deserving estate agents' secretaries.

From *Professor Branestawm's Perilous Pudding*

How to Push Your
Friend Through a
One-Centimetre Hole

Cut a hole a centimetre in diameter in a piece of cardboard, then choose a nice fat friend and say you can push him through this hole. He will say you can't do it, but by Professor Branestawm's special friend-pushing method you can. Just hold the card close to him, put your little finger through the hole and push him. You've pushed him through a one-centimetre hole.

In case he thinks that's cheating, offer to pass yourself through a postcard.

You can really do this and you don't need a giant postcard either. Take an ordinary postcard and fold it exactly in halves lengthways down the middle. Open the card out again and with a Stanley 99 knife cut a slit through the card along the fold to within about 1 cm of each end, as in Figure 1. Refold the card, carefully so that it doesn't come apart, and then with

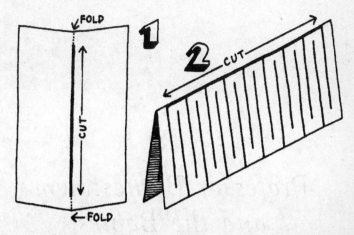

a pair of scissors make a lot of cuts almost across the card and close together, as shown in Figure 2. Make the cuts alternately from the folded edge and the other edge. When you have finished you will find you can open out the postcard very carefully so that it is big enough for you to pass it over your head and down to the ground so that you can step through it.

From *Professor Branestawm's Do-It-Yourself Handbook*

Professor Branestawm and the Babies

Professor Branestawm looked at the baby over the top of all five of his pairs of spectacles.

The baby looked at the Professor over the top of his mum's back. His mum patted him on his own back.

'I, ah, hullo,' said the Professor.

'Burp,' said the baby, blew a small bubble and added, 'G-e-e-e-e.'

'That's got it,' said mum, who in fact was Mrs Flittersnoop's sister Aggie's cousin Ada from North Pagwell, who had brought her nice new baby to show off.

You might not think there was anything in that to set the Professor off on a new invention. But it was one of those days, and before Mrs Flittersnoop and cousin Ada were half-way through their fourth cups of tea, the Professor was nine-tenths of the way through a highly twiddly device for helping babies to burp better.

'You know how one gets the gurgly noises in the water pipes at times,' he said to Dr Mumpzanmeazle, who had called in to see that the baby was in good running order. 'Well, it's the same kind of thing. A baby's, um, ah, windies are caused by a sort of air lock in the pipes.'

'Of course,' said Dr Mumpzanmeazle, waving his stethoscope about and knocking the Professor's glasses into the gluepot, which fortunately contained only a clean handkerchief the Professor had put there by mistake instead of in his pocket. They were in the Professor's inventory. The walls were covered with little pink doggies and blue bunnies which Mrs Flittersnoop had stuck there to help the baby atmosphere.

And on the bench stood the Professor's Baby Burper its own self. It looked like a toy steamroller with three funnels, but not very much like one.

'When you press down this lever,' explained the Professor, 'an electronic movement is set up which releases the, er, wind in the baby's . . .'

'Exactly,' cried Dr Mumpzanmeazle, who knew all about wind in a baby's plumbing. He shot off into a great deal of doctorish talk about tubes and digestive thingummies. The Professor's head began to go round and round, just as Colonel Dedshott's always did when the Professor explained things to him.

'You follow, Professor?' asked the Doctor.

'Quite, quite,' said the Professor, who hadn't been listening as he had just thought of a sort of optional extra attachment for his invention, to make it cure hiccups; with a further attachment, five times larger than the machine itself, for preventing milk boiling over.

Dr Mumpzanmeazle shot off to see somebody about some spots, and in walked Mrs Flittersnoop's cat, who had just finished a king-size saucer of milk. 'Brr, brr,' said the cat, jumping up on the bench and rubbing himself against the Baby Burper, which promptly went 'Tweet, tweet.' The cat said, 'Burp'. Then as he didn't agree with having his windies brought up without his permission, gave the machine a dirty look and stalked out with becoming dignity.

The Professor had arranged to demonstrate his Baby Burper at the Pagwell Baby Clinic. He wrapped it up in some fancy paper covered in pansies and baby ducks, left it on the hall table, came back for it and left his hat on the hall chair. Then he came back for that, forgot where he was going and finally arrived at the Pagwell Baby Clinic by getting on the wrong bus, thinking he was going to Pagwell Zoo, which happened to be the right bus for going to Pagwell Baby Clinic.

'We shall be most interested to see your invention, Professor,' said the Matron, smiling with all her teeth at once and folding her hands over her waist as far as they would go, which wasn't very far as she was considerably on the large side.

'The babies have been fed?' enquired the Professor, unwrapping his invention. Dr Mumpzanmeazle had impressed on him that it couldn't bring up a baby's windies if he hadn't got any windies to bring up. 'Best time is just after a feed,' he said. It was this being concerned with feeding time that had almost led the Professor to the Zoo. Thank goodness he didn't get there because of what might happen if you make an enormous elephant burp.

'This wheel', said the Professor, holding up the invention with the air of someone selling cough mixture, 'can be turned according to the size, duration and strength of burp required.'

'According to the size of feed consumed,' added the Matron, nodding to the row of mums who had come to have their babies de-burped.

'And here', went on the Professor, 'is an adjustable thingummy arranger for using the machine on grown ups after such things as, er . . .'

'Christmas parties and summertime outdoor blowouts,' said one of the mums.

'Precisely,' said the Professor. He aimed the machine at the first baby in the line, and pressed the lever. 'Tweet,' said the machine and, 'Burp,' said the baby. Everyone was delighted.

'Saves all that back slapping,' said another mum, who had had triplets and been given rather an overdose of back-slapping herself in consequence.

Burp, burp, burpetty burp. The Professor moved down the line with his invention. The demonstration was being a roaring success. Then he put down the Baby Burper while he blew his nose. A little boy with red hair, who had got his head stuck in a pink plastic toddy pot that didn't go with it at all, came crawling along and bumped into the Burper, which promptly resented it.

Tweet, tweet! Burp! Plot! Plonk!

The little boy burped a grown-up sized burp, the toddy pot flew off his head and landed on a little girl who was playing with a blue teddy bear and giving no trouble up to then. 'Gururururururg!' she shouted and threw the teddy bear at the Professor, missed him by half a room width but scored a direct hit on a tray of tea a nurse was bringing in for the mums.

Crash, sloshety bang! Clinical china was all over the place. Steam went up. The nurse who was scared of the Matron at the best of times, leapt into a play pen and tried to hide under a heap of striped woolly balls. One baby who was rather a late feeder pulled the top off her feeding bottle and poured the contents over the Professor's head.

'Pwouff!' he gasped, blowing valuable vitamins all over the linoleum.

Then the Baby Burper really got out of hand.

Burp burp, double burp, burpy burpetty burp!, all the babies broke out in windie-upping. The Professor made a dash for his machine and fell over a set of triplets who were burping in waltz time.

The Matron opened her mouth to give severe orders but it was immediately filled with high quality, double-sterilized cotton wool thrown by a rather elderly baby who had climbed on to the mantelpiece to get a better aim.

Tweet tweet, tweetie tweet, went the Baby Burper, careering round the clinic with all levers pressed.

Burping broke out among the mums, who seemed to do it even better than the babies. Soprano burps and treble burps and contralto burps came rolling out. It sounded like a Wurlitzer organ with energetic hiccups.

'Oh dear!' groaned the Professor. 'And I thought this was going to be such a nice quiet little invention that couldn't cause any uproar.' He clutched his five pairs of spectacles and tried to catch his machine.

'Stop this at, burp, once,' exploded the Matron.

Out in the street Colonel Dedshott was striding past on his way to a Regimental Tea Party of the Catapult Cavaliers, when a window of the clinic burst open and someone shouted, 'Help . . . burp!'

'By Jove, what!' exclaimed the Colonel deciding that Regimental Tea Parties must give place to rescuing people who needed help. 'Coming, my word, what!'

He dashed up to a door but it was marked 'Nurses only'. The Colonel's military mind instantly rose to the occasion. He dashed into a draper's shop that happened to be standing by and bought a nurse's cap and apron.

'To the rescue!' he cried, and with the apron on upside down and the cap tied on top of his Catapult Cavaliers special dress hat, worn only for Regimental Tea Parties, he pushed open the door and rushed up the stairs.

Burp burp, burpetty burp!, a machine-gun fire of windies met him. Seven mums tried to drape themselves round his neck. The baby on the mantelpiece opened fire with highly absorbent cotton wool balls.

Tweet tweet tweet.
Burp burpetty, bang pop burp.
Down below two policemen looked up at the noise.

'I never did hold with these clinic places,' said one.

'Nor me neither,' said the other and they went off to find a nice quiet burglary to attend to.

'Rescue!' roared Colonel Dedshott, brandishing his catapult. He looked wildly round at the assortment of burping babies. 'Ha, diddums then, by Jove! Stop it there, ickle sweetie pie!'

For once even Colonel Dedshott was defeated. For how can even the bravest soldier contend with armies of babies? What can you do with an enemy that giggles and burps when you threaten him? What indeed!

'Help, Dedshott!' gasped the Professor from under a set of babies who were crawling over him with rattles waving.

Colonel Dedshott took aim with his catapult at the burping machine that was trying to climb up the Matron's leg. *Plonk*, he missed. The bullet bounced off the floor and hit the fire alarm bell.

'Clang-a-lang-a-lang!' yelled the bell.

'Tweetie tweet tweet,' squeaked the Baby Burper.

'Burp.' 'By gad, sir!' 'Help!' 'Burpie burp.'

Then the Matron slipped on some vitamin-activated ointment someone had spilt on the floor, and sat on the machine, which gave an agonised squeal and went flat.

Instantly the burping stopped. The mums grabbed their babies while the grabbing was good. Colonel Dedshott grabbed the Professor. They shot down the stairs just in time to meet the Great Pagwell Fire Brigade, who weren't needed for any fires but came in very handy for getting the Professor and the Colonel away from the battlefield.

So Colonel Dedshott arrived on the fire engine almost in time for his Regimental Tea Party, which meant he was in time for the cake but didn't have to eat bread and butter first, which the Army is usually very strict about soldiers doing. But as he had forgotten to take off the nurse's apron, he nearly got himself mixed up with the washing-up.

And Professor Branestawm was delivered safely home to Mrs Flittersnoop, a bit out of breath. 'In future I shall, er, avoid babies,' he gasped, collapsing into a chair which collapsed as well because it had only three legs and was waiting to be mended, 'Babies, I feel, are, er, somewhat dangerous.'

'Yes, indeed, I'm sure, sir,' said Mrs Flittersnoop. She helped the Professor into a more complete chair and went back to the roly-poly she was making for dinner, which would probably be quite capable of producing a burp or two itself without the help of any sensational inventions.

But it was a jolly good job Professor Branestawm was never likely to have any babies of his own, who might need servicing, so to speak. Because the Matron of the Pagwell Baby Clinic definitely went off him in a big way after the hoo-haa his invention had caused, and whenever she met him in the street she looked the other way as if she hadn't seen him. But as he almost certainly would be too soaked up in a new invention to notice her, nothing really mattered much.

From *The Peculiar Triumph of Professor Branestawm*

Professor Branestawm's
Secret Book of Plans

Professor Branestawm keeps a book of plans for his inventions. But he keeps the plans secret because his book is a specially invented one and if anyone looks in it all they see is blank paper.

To demonstrate this to your friends, you show them a book and flip over the pages and they are all seen to be quite blank.

But, of course, when the Professor wants to consult his plans he can always see them in the book. And so you flip the pages again, and each page has on it a diagram for an invention.

To make this magic book you want a number of pieces of fairly stiff white paper cut to about 8 cm by 10 cm. Fasten them all together along one of the long edges with paper fasteners pushed through and bent over. If you like, the two outer pieces of paper can be coloured paper, to make a cover for the book.

Now go through the book and cut every other page about 3 mm or so shorter than the others, cutting along the long side of the book.

Go through the book again and on each short page draw a diagram of an invention. You can copy some of the machines from the Professor Branestawm stories, or invent some of your own.

You will now find that if you hold the book in your left hand and riffle the pages with the other hand, the short pages will go past without the diagrams being seen. To make the diagrams appear, flick the pages the other way, holding the book in your right hand and riffling the pages with your left. The diagrams will then appear.

Figures 1 and 2 show how to make the book and use it.

You can, of course, make this book from an ordinary notebook, by cutting every other page short. But you may find it difficult to get a suitable book with opaque paper. And if the paper isn't opaque the diagrams will show through the paper and be seen when they shouldn't.

From *Professor Branestawm's Do-It-Yourself Handbook*

<hr>

Why were Professor Branestawm's socks beaten when he took them off?
Because they were de-feated.

Professor Branestawm Round the Bend

Professor Branestawm came carefully downstairs backwards. This, of course, was the kind of thing the Professor was apt to do, either because he thought he was going upstairs, or because he had his mind on a new invention, or even because he had caught the habit from his next-door neighbour, Commander Hardaport (Retired). Commander Hardaport was an exceedingly naval gentleman, and always came downstairs backwards because sailors have to do that on ships in case of rough seas and because ships' staircases are rather on the vertical side.

But this time was different. The Professor had had a slight accident with an extra truculent invention and had hurt his foot so that he couldn't get down steps unless he did it backwards.

'I am, er, ah, going to Pagwell University this

morning,' he said to Mrs Flittersnoop, who was laying the breakfast table, 'to deliver a lecture on . . . er, that is to say, I am speaking to them about . . .' He realized he couldn't remember what he was going to lecture about, consulted his notes but found they were diagrams for an invention for special ink that always spelt words correctly, and then discovered he had written the subject of his lecture on a paper serviette. It was one of Mrs Flittersnoop's best, double-thickness, super-strength ones that she kept for visitors but she didn't mind as she felt it was in a good cause.

'Yes, indeed, I'm sure, sir,' she said, deftly moving the Professor's fried egg out of the way before he put his teacup down on it. 'Will you be in to lunch, sir?'

'I, er, yes, of course, don't mention it,' said the Professor. He spread marmalade on his fried egg, put salt in his tea, put his hat on the wrong way round and went out.

He arrived at Great Pagwell Station just in time to miss the train before his, which was just as well because he would almost certainly have got on it and it wasn't going anywhere near where he wanted to go.

'Is this my train?' he asked the Station-master, as another train came rattling and zooming in.

'No, it is not,' said the Station-master, deciding to be a bit funny as it was a fine day. 'This train belongs to the Railway Company.'

'Oh, um,' said the Professor. 'Then I am sure they will not mind my using it.'

'Of course, Professor,' said the Station-master. 'Allow me to help you in. Dear, dear, whatever have you done to your foot?'

'An, um, er, slight accident with an invention,' said the Professor. 'That is why I am travelling by train instead of by car, because I find it somewhat, er, difficult to operate the foot levers of the integrating clutch system of my car.'

'Quite, quite,' said the Station-master, giving the Professor a final push into the carriage.

He waved his hands. The passengers waved back thinking what a nice man he was to be so friendly. Something made a buzzing noise somewhere and the train drew out of the station with the Professor sitting tidily in a carriage, on the seat, not up on the rack or in the luggage-van or anywhere else he could easily have been as he was so absent-minded.

He started thinking about new inventions. He thought of self-eating rice pudding for people who didn't like it. He pondered over non-sticky glue to keep your fingers clean, and considered the possibility of invisible paint that wouldn't show if you spilt it on the carpet.

And he was so busy thinking of incredible new inventions he only just noticed in time that the train had stopped at a station.

'Er, um, ha, here I am,' he said. He opened the door and began slowly getting out of the carriage backwards because of course with his bad foot he couldn't get out forwards.

But, oh dear, the porters thought he was getting *into* the train and, being nice helpful railway porters, they shouted, 'Hurry along there!' and gave him a helpful push back into the carriage and shut the door.

'I, er, thank you very much but I wish to, er,' he stuttered. But the train was already off to stations new.

It was a good thing for the Professor that that station was Upper Pagwell, where he didn't have to get out for the University. Because if it had been Pagwell North, where he did have to get out, he would have been carried past his station. On the other hand if he hadn't had a bad foot, which he couldn't have had on either hand if it comes to that, he would have got out at the wrong station as usual and Pagwell University would have been deprived of his lecture.

The Professor sank back on to the seat and went on thinking of disastrous new inventions. He was half-way to thinking of an astounding method for making coal from sawdust and potato peelings when the train pulled into Pagwell North.

'Ha!' said the Professor, coming out of his inventing thoughts. 'This is where I get out.'

He started getting out of the train backwards as before, but again a helpful porter came dashing up to help him. And, of course, once again he thought the Professor was trying to get into the train, not out of it. And once again he helped him back into his carriage.

'But I wish to, er, that is to say, I do not wish, er, um, at least, this is where I . . .' he spluttered.

'That's all right, sir,' shouted the porter. 'You're all

*An astounding method for making coal
from sawdust and potato peelings*

right now, sir. Hold tight,' and with a lot of flag-waving and buzzing and hand-signalling the train steamed out of the station, or it would have done if only it had been a steam train and not a diesel electric one.

'Dear me, this is most awkward,' grunted the Professor, clashing his spectacles about a bit as the train went zooming off. 'Now I shall have to get out at the next station and catch a bus back. That is to say, if there is a bus. Otherwise I shall have to catch another train back to Pagwell North and that will mean crossing the line by the footbridge, which will, I am afraid, be, um, er, rather difficult with a bad foot.'

Houses and telegraph poles and people's gardens went streaming past and presently the train slowed down and stopped at Pagwell-by-Poppingford. The Professor started climbing out, backwards again of course because it was the only way he could get out.

'Pagwellpoppord!' shouted a porter, which was the railway porters' short way of saying Pagwell-by-Poppingford, only it was so short none of the passengers could understand it except one who used to be a railway porter himself and knew where he was anyway.

But Professor Branestawm didn't care where it was. He only wanted to get out of the train so as to get back to Pagwell North to give his lecture at the University.

'Hurry along there, please!' shouted the porters, and they came running up and helped the Professor most politely back into his carriage, thinking, as the other porters had done, that he was trying to get in. And off went the train again carrying the Professor farther and farther from where he wanted to be.

'Tut, tut, I shall never get there in time to give my lecture,' gasped the Professor. He pulled the alarm chain without bothering how much it was going to cost, but it came off in his hand. He leaned out of the window even though there were severe notices saying he mustn't.

On went the train. *Errk*, it snorted through tunnels. *Zimzimetty zim*, it rattled across switches. *Rm-m-m*, it zoomed over bridges. Other people's houses and other people's gardens and other people's dogs and cats and flowers and vegetables shot past at high speed. People who had no lectures to give at Universities were overtaken and left behind.

Pagwell Muffington came and went. The train stopped at Pretty Pagwell, Pagwell-on-the-Hill and Pagwell Road. But each time the Professor tried to get out the porters thought he was getting in, because he tried to get out backwards. And each time they helped him back and the train went on.

'Oh dear, I shall never get anywhere like this,' groaned the Professor. 'I shall never be able to get out of this train. I shall starve to death. Oh, oh, oh!'

At Pagwell University they were looking at their watches, gazing at the clocks and checking the time with the invisible lady on the telephone.

'What can have happened to Professor Branestawm?' they said. But they knew so many things could have happened to the Professor and probably had, it wasn't much use guessing.

'Ring up his home,' said the Dean, 'and find out if he's been delayed or forgotten about the lecture or got himself immersed in an invention.'

Mrs Flittersnoop said oh yes indeed, the Professor had left in good time. But after the University man had rung off she was a bit worried and so she called Colonel Dedshott of the Catapult Cavaliers. He was the Professor's extra special friend, always ready to have his head made to go round and round listening to the Professor explaining an invention, or to go dashing off in several directions to rescue the Professor from dangers or help him out of fixes. He got his Catapult Cavaliers out to see if they could find where the Professor had gone. They started by enquiring at all the railway stations, with photos of the Professor, to find out if anyone like him had got on the train. And at the very first station they asked, Great Pagwell, the Station-master and porters said, oh yes, definitely, the Professor had got on at Great Pagwell.

But, oh goodness, the porter at Pagwell North said he had got on there too. And at Pagwell-by-Poppingford they said he had got on there. And the same at Pagwell Muffington, Pretty Pagwell, Pagwell-on-the-Hill and Pagwell Road.

'Ha, nonsense, by Jove!' grunted Colonel Dedshott. 'Professor's a clever chap, of course, but can't have got on a train at *all* these stations. My word, perhaps some villains are impersonating him.' But as the Colonel couldn't think of even an unlikely reason why anyone should want to impersonate the Professor that didn't help.

'Do you think perhaps the Professor has invented a thing that has accidentally split him into a dozen Professors?' enquired Mrs Flittersnoop, hoping very much it was impossible, but you had to consider everything, hadn't you?

Soon word came in from Pagwell Woods, Pagwell Green and Pagwell Junction that the Professor had been seen getting on a train at all these stations. But, of course, what he had really been seen doing was trying to get *off* the train. Everybody thought he was trying to get on and helped him in.

'If only someone else would get in this carriage,' groaned the Professor. 'Then I could tell them I wanted to get out.'

But nobody did get in because it was one of those slow trains that stop at every possible station and in between as well if it can, and so nobody got on it unless they only wanted to go to the next station, and none of them got in the Professor's carriage because he was always in the way trying to get out. And anyway, thought the Professor, what was the use at this stage? If he had managed to get out of the train at some far-off place like Pagwell Woods he would have got in such a muddle trying to get back to Pagwell North he might have been worse off than he was now, where at least he was under cover if it rained.

The Catapult Cavaliers continued diligently showing photos of the Professor all round to see if he had been seen anywhere and kept finding he had been seen getting on a train at nearly every station the railway had in stock.

Meanwhile the Dean of Pagwell University was getting annoyed. 'Here I have all the students assembled, that is to say all except those who couldn't come because of illness or wouldn't come because they didn't care for lectures or haven't come because of some other reason, and no Professor Branestawm and therefore no lecture.'

'That sounds quite logical to me,' said the Assistant Dean, shaking biscuit crumbs out of his gown because he had just had his coffee break. 'And perhaps less embarrassing for us than if Professor Branestawm had arrived and no students had turned up to listen to his lecture.'

'Pah!' snorted the Dean, which is a rather un-University thing to snort. 'We shall have to think up something for the students to do now they're here.'

'How about party games?' suggested the Assistant Dean.

'Party games!' screeched the Dean, cramming his mortar-board down over his ears. 'Party games at a University? Whoever heard of such a thing?'

'Well, I did just now,' said the Assistant Dean, 'when I mentioned it, and again when you objected to it.'

'*Pah*, all over again!' cried the Dean. 'You go and lecture to the students to keep them quiet while I ring the Professor's house again.'

So the Assistant Dean went off and lectured to the students, which didn't keep them quiet at all because they were disappointed at not hearing a lecture from Professor Branestawm.

The train with Professor Branestawm still unwillingly in it went rattling on. It stopped at Pagwell Halt, at Pagwell Halfpenny, Pagwell Hill and Pagwell Bridge. And the Professor didn't manage to get out at any of them, partly because the porters at each station thought he was trying to get in and partly because he had almost given up hope of ever getting out of that train.

Presently the train stopped at another station.

'It seems hardly worthwhile trying to get out,' moaned the Professor. Then he said, 'Good gracious, how very strange! This station seems familiar. Surely, I, um, recognize that machine that sells you sausage-flavoured crisps if you put the right coin in the right slot and the machine isn't empty. And I, er, believe I recognize that sign saying "Lost Property". I've always wondered how it could be lost if they knew where it was. Dear me, can I have been here before?'

Yes, he could have and he had. For, strange surprise, the train had arrived back at Great Pagwell station! That part of the line went round the various Pagwells in a railway circle and came back to where it started.

'Well,' groaned the Professor, when he finally realized where he was, 'I've heard of people going round the bend, but this is really going too far round it. If I don't manage to get out here I'm imprisoned for life in a train. Wonderful headline for the papers but most, um, ah, inconvenient for me.'

But it was all right. The Station-master at Great Pagwell of course knew about the Professor's bad foot and helped him to get out of the train. Then he charged him the fare from Pagwell North right round the outer circle and back to Great Pagwell, which seems a bit unfair but railways are very strict about passengers travelling without paying, even if they don't particularly want to travel.

The telephone was ringing as Professor Branestawm crept wearily into his house. It was the Dean of Pagwell University who had just managed to get on to the Professor's house again after getting connected to the fire station, the dairy, and the Home for Lost Squirrels by mistake.

'Ah, Professor!' cried the Dean. 'We were expecting you at the University to give your lecture.'

'Um, ah, yes,' said the Professor, and he explained what had happened, which made the Dean's head go round and round nearly as fast as Colonel Dedshott's did at the Professor's explanations, but not nearly as fast as the train had gone round with the Professor shut up in it.

'I think it would be better,' said the Dean, 'if we brought the students to you to save you coming here with your bad foot.'

'Er, um, ah yes, quite so,' said the Professor, not seeing how he could get to the University *without* his bad foot as he was rather attached to it.

So the students from Pagwell University crammed into the Professor's sitting-room with some standing in corners and some sitting on the bookshelves, which seemed a suitable place for students to sit. And Mrs Flittersnoop came up with tea and home-made scones all round.

And Professor Branestawm was at last able to give his notable lecture on the efficient and economical way to use the railway.

From *Professor Branestawm Round the Bend*

A policeman stopped Professor Branestawm in his car and said he had been doing fifty miles an hour in a forty mile an hour zone. The Professor said that wasn't possible. Why not?
Because he had been out for only half an hour.

Everything Handy

A place for everything and nothing in its place. That's what you usually find in Professor Branestawm's inventory. But of course it's different at home, isn't it? Well, it can be now, for here is Professor Branestawm's idea for where to keep all the odds and ends and bits of nonsense Mum has to have handy in the kitchen or Dad wouldn't mind if he had in the workshop or they wish you had in your room instead of all over the house.

All you need is a number of empty jam jars – the kind that have a twist-off lid. When you've eaten the jam – and they don't give you the instructions for this on the label – screw the lids to the *underside* of a shelf, fixing them a little way apart. Now all you have to do is put the jar up into the lid, give it a twist and it's fixed. Whenever you need the sugar, or salt, or little skinny screws, or long nails, or anything else, you just

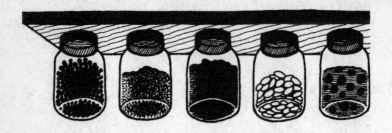

take the jar that contains them, give it a twist and it comes free in your hand. Only one hand is needed, so you can use the other for knocking over the milk or getting it caught in the egg whisk or any other useful job.

And, of course, you can always find what you want because the glass jars let you see what's in them. No labels needed, which is handy, too, if your spelling isn't up to much.

From *Professor Branestawm's Do-It-Yourself Handbook*

Branestawm's
Portable Car Park

Professor Branestawm came out of Great Pagwell Town Hall to find a very large lady traffic warden standing by his car and glaring at it as if it was something the dustmen preferred not to take away. And it certainly looked as if it would resent being taken away by dustmen, being a special invention of the Professor's, with six wheels, two engines, a television set and a photo of the Mayor inside the bonnet.

'Are you driving this car?' she asked the Professor.

'Well, no, I'm not,' said the Professor.

'Then who is?' asked the traffic warden.

'Er, ah, nobody is driving it,' said the Professor, looking at the warden through various pairs of spectacles.

Car abandoned, wrote the traffic warden, in a fierce notebook. Then the Professor got into the car and started both engines.

'I thought you said this wasn't your car,' growled the traffic warden, crossing out what she'd written.

'Er, no, I didn't say that,' said the Professor. 'I said I was not driving it, but I am now going to do so.' He pulled a lever and the car slid sideways out of its parking space. He pressed a button and the car shot off down the street, while the traffic warden, who tried to clap a parking ticket on it, clapped it on the Mayor's car instead, which was parked just behind.

Of course, the Professor shouldn't have parked his car there at all because it was the space specially reserved for the Mayor's car. The Mayor had had to park his car behind, where there was a 'No parking' notice, and so it really deserved the parking ticket the traffic warden awarded it. But she thought there might be a bit of a scandal if the Mayor was summonsed for parking outside his own Town Hall, and she tried to scrape the parking ticket off. And Pagwell's newest policeman nearly arrested her for trying to remove a parking ticket illegally.

'I shall have to do something about this car parking business,' said the Professor to Mrs Flittersnoop when he got home, too late for lunch and too early for tea. 'Wherever I go there are notices saying "No parking" and "No stopping" and "No entry" until really the only way to avoid breaking the law is to drive to where one wants to go, then drive straight home again without stopping and walk back.'

'You could take a bus, I suppose, sir,' said Mrs Flittersnoop, always willing to be helpful.

'There are severe penalties for taking buses or

other municipal property,' said the Professor. 'And anyway, where could I park a bus if I can't park my car? No, I shall find a way of parking my car where I please without breaking the law. And I have an idea how I can do it.' He put on his hat and went out.

Professor Branestawm was on his way to Great Pagwell Library, when he came upon a large crowd of people.

'I'm afraid you'll have to go round another way,' said a policeman to the Professor. 'Someone's been knocked down by the library.'

'Have they really?' said the Professor. 'I had no idea libraries attacked people.' And he drove off down a side turning.

'I shall go to Pagwell Gardens Library,' said the Professor to himself. 'That's a nice quiet library.'

But, whether it was a nice quiet library or not, there was no space for the Professor to park his car and there were rows of traffic wardens brandishing parking tickets and waiting to pounce on him. So he went home again, arriving too late for tea and too early for supper.

'I'm going to Pagwell Gardens Library,' he said to Mrs Flittersnoop. 'And I shall go by train, which is much easier as one does not have to find anywhere to park a train.'

He got out of the train at Pagwell Gardens station and saw a large notice printed in British Rail's best black letters.

'Passengers MUST cross the line by the footbridge,' it said.

'Um,' said the Professor, and, as he was always careful to obey notices, he crossed the line by the footbridge.

When he got to the other side he was met by another notice, just like the first, saying 'Passengers MUST cross the line by the footbridge.'

'Well, I've just done that,' he said. 'But I suppose these British Rail people know best what is safe to do on a railway.' So he turned round and went back across the footbridge.

But when he got back there was the first notice, still saying that passengers MUST cross the line by the footbridge. It was quite firm about it.

'Oh dear, I am really afraid I shall have to disobey the rule,' muttered the Professor. He was just going to walk out of the station instead of crossing the line by the footbridge when Pagwell's newest policeman appeared.

'Now he's going to say, "What's all this? Why aren't you crossing the line by the footbridge as the notice says?"' thought the Professor.

But the policeman said, 'Excuse me, sir, I'm new here. Can you direct me to the police station?'

'Certainly,' said the Professor, in his best law-abiding manner. 'Come this way, constable.' He walked straight past the footbridge notice and out into the streets of Pagwell Gardens, followed by the policeman.

'Take the first on the left and the third on the right,' said the Professor. 'And that will lead you to the police station.'

'Thank you very much, sir,' said the policeman.

And off he went.

The Professor's directions didn't lead to the police station at all, but to the library. The Professor realized that he couldn't remember the way to the library himself and so he had to ask a passer-by who turned out to be a stranger to the place, and he directed the Professor to the police station instead of the library. But fortunately the Professor went the wrong way as usual and arrived at the library just as the new policeman he had misdirected to the police station arrived at the library as well.

Luckily there was a car parked the wrong way round in a no-parking area during prohibited hours and obstructing the entrance to the car park. So that attracted the attention of the new policeman, and the Professor got into the library without any trouble, except from the revolving doors, which whizzed him round so that he kept coming out of the library instead of going into it.

But at last he was safely inside, and was asking for *The Bye-Laws, Rules and Regulations of the Rural Borough of Great Pagwell.* It told you all the things you mustn't do, and so it was a very thick book.

'Traffic Regulations,' said the Professor, turning pages. 'Um, yes, here we are.'

The Great Pagwell Traffic Regulations included some from the Highway Code and some original ones of Great Pagwell's Council. They told you you mustn't park a car on the brow of a hill, at a bus stop, traffic lights or pedestrian crossing, alongside another vehicle or by road works. And they also told you, by courtesy of the Great Pagwell Council, that you could 'park a vehicle without charge in any approved car park in the Rural Borough of Great Pagwell' and it added very helpfully, 'A car park should be any place where cars may be parked and such shall be designated by a notice inscribed "Car Park".'

'Um, that seems clear enough,' said the Professor.

It was another day in Great Pagwell. And although it looked much the same as any day, this was an exceedingly special day.

For it was the day on which Professor Branestawm had decided to try out his wonderfully ingenious and incredibly simple Portable Car Park.

'But you can't have a portable car park!' exploded Commander Hardaport (Retired) when the Professor told him about it. 'Car parks are whacking great pieces of ground! You can't go carrying them about.'

'I can carry my car park about,' said the Professor, and he set off for Great Pagwell to find somewhere to park his car in his portable car park.

He drew up in the High Street, opposite Ginnibag & Knitwoddle's store. There were two yellow lines along the kerb, and three policemen and two traffic wardens watching them.

The Professor stepped out of his car, raised his hat politely to the traffic wardens, who were ladies, but not to the policemen, who were not. Then he walked away.

'Excuse me, sir!' 'Just a minute, please!' 'You can't do that here!' 'Come back!' shouted the policemen and the wardens like a grand opera chorus.

'Were you speaking to me?' asked the Professor, very politely. 'Yes, we were,' they said. 'You can't leave that car there. It's a no-parking area.'

'Ah, pardon me,' said the Professor. 'But I have every right to park here. This is a car park,' and he pointed to a tall pole carrying a board that said in large capital letters CAR PARK.

'You just put that pole there yourself,' said one of the policemen.

'That doesn't make this a car park,' said one of the wardens, getting out a packet of parking tickets and several pencils.

'This', said the Professor, waving spectacles about in the wind, '*is* the Rural Borough of Great Pagwell, I believe?'

'Of course it is,' said a policeman.

'Then my car is parked in an approved car park within the meaning of the bye-laws,' said the Professor, arranging his spectacles in a different order and smiling at the policeman.

'Nonsense, this is a prohibited area,' said the policeman. 'And you've no right to erect that pole neither.'

'A car park,' said the Professor, quoting the bye-laws very carefully as he had learnt them by heart, 'a car park shall be any place where cars may be parked and such shall be designated by a notice inscribed "Car Park". And there is the notice,' finished the Professor, pointing triumphantly at his sign.

By this time five more cars, two delivery vans and a truck full of ironwork had parked themselves behind the Professor's car and his 'Car Park' notice.

The three policeman and the two wardens stared in amazement.

'I think that has established my legal right to use my portable car park,' said the Professor. He got into his car and drove off, taking the pole with him, and immediately the two traffic wardens started joyfully giving out parking tickets to all the vehicles that had parked behind the Professor, while the policemen got into their police car and went whizzing off, with the horn going *bar-bur, bar-bur*, to catch the Professor.

Along Pagwell High Street shot the Professor. He came to a roundabout and drove on to it with the police car in hot and noisy pursuit. He turned off the roundabout, and found the road led into another roundabout. He turned off that and found himself in a third roundabout.

'Oh dear, this is worse than the footbridge at Pagwell Gardens Station,' he cried, going round and round the roundabout, not knowing where to turn off in case it took him into another roundabout. Then he saw a sign that said 'City Centre', and so he turned into that with the police car close behind him, and found himself back at the first roundabout.

'I shall never get out of this,' he murmured.

He turned left at the next exit but that took him back to the roundabout he had just come off.

'This is terrible!' he cried. 'I used to like going on roundabouts when I was little, but they were different. They had music, and horses . . . Good gracious! What's that?'

He had no sooner said the word 'music' than music broke out on the roundabout, and then horses appeared.

It was a detachment of the Catapult Cavaliers, with their band led by Colonel Dedshott, on their way to help the Mayor open a new hospital. The Professor had managed to get into the middle of a Municipal Procession. The police car, carefully giving way to vehicles already on the roundabout, finished up behind the Mayor's car and the policeman driver was watching so carefully to avoid running into the Mayor that he lost sight of the Professor.

Meanwhile the Professor had seen Colonel Dedshott.

'Dedshott!' he shouted. 'Help, Dedshott!'

'Hrrmp!' cried the Colonel. He yelled commands and stopped the horses and the band half-way round the roundabout. He didn't know whether there was a law saying that you mustn't stop a troop of horse soldiers with their band on a roundabout, but he wasn't going to leave his old friend Professor Branestawm in the lurch.

'My word, Branestawm, in trouble, what?' he shouted, cantering up to the Professor.

'I am afraid I have lost the way, Dedshott,' said the Professor.

'Ha!' grunted the Colonel. 'Follow us, Branestawm, soon have you out of this.'

He gave commands to the Catapult Cavaliers, and on they swept, out of one roundabout into the next, out of that and down the road that led past the hospital where the Mayor and his party were just arriving.

'Thank you very much, Dedshott,' called the Professor, very much relieved.

He drove past the hospital, down the street and parked his car outside Ye Olde Bunne Shoppe. There were five yellow lines painted along the kerb, which meant nobody must ever leave a car within miles of the place, but the Professor just erected his portable car park sign beside his car and went in to have a quiet cup of tea and some fishpaste sandwiches to recover from his exhausting afternoon.

Meanwhile the policemen had also managed to escape from the Mayor's procession. They had gone off to call a meeting to see if they could get a law passed saying that nobody must park a car anywhere, not even in a car park, in case it happened to be Professor Branestawm's portable car park. And so large numbers of policemen and traffic wardens were driving around looking for somewhere to hold their meeting, when they saw a sign saying 'Car Park' outside Ye Olde Bunne Shoppe, and decided that that would be a good place to go in case all that thinking made them hungry.

They parked their cars under what they thought was a genuine, hundred per cent, regulation car park sign, and everyone went in for tea and buns and thinking.

They had no sooner gone in than the Professor came out, full of tea and sandwiches and half a paper napkin he had eaten by mistake. And he took his car away together with his portable car park sign, leaving all the official cars illegally parked on yellow lines.

But, as usual, everything worked out for the best

because when the policemen and traffic wardens came out, they got involved in such a complicated, legal argument as to whether they should give one another tickets for parking on yellow lines, that they forgot all about trying to arrest the Professor. And in the excitement of being rescued from the roundabouts by horses, the Professor had lost interest in his portable car park and had gone home to work on an even more shattering invention, a portable subway for making it safer to cross the road at roundabouts.

From *Professor Branestawm's Great Revolution*

A Finder of Lost Things

Professor Branestawm once invented an astonishing machine for finding his spectacles when he lost them, which was often. This device for finding lost things isn't as complicated as the Professor's machine, but on the other hand it isn't likely to go wild and purposely lose things so that it can find them again, as the Professor's machine did.

This wonderful thing is in fact nothing more than an ordinary magnet. You fasten the magnet to a long wooden stick or cane by binding it on with sticky tape, as shown in Figure 1. Or you could get Dad to drill a hole in the loop part of the magnet and then fasten the magnet to the stick with a little screw.

Now if you have lost some small thing made of iron or steel, the magnet will find it for you. Suppose you have dropped your sewing needle on a patterned carpet. You'll never find it by looking but just pass your magnet along the floor and soon, *click*, the needle will attach itself to the magnet. Suppose you drop a small but highly vital little screw in the workshop, all among the sawdust and shavings. Draw your magnet along the floor and the little screw will pop out and stick to the magnet.

You actually could use this device for finding needles in haystacks. That is, supposing needles ever really got lost in haystacks and as long as the farmer didn't mind your pulling the haystack to bits, which he probably would.

Oh, don't forget to keep a piece of steel, such as a thick nail, across the ends of the magnet when you're not using it. This is called a 'keeper' and prevents the magnet from losing its magnetism.

From *Professor Branestawm's Do-It-Yourself Handbook*

The Screaming Clocks

I'm going to write some letters for an hour and I'm not to be disturbed,' said the Professor to Mrs Flittersnoop, arranging his five pairs of glasses nice and neatly on his forehead for when he wanted to use them, 'and I'll have a cup of tea when I've finished.'

'Yes, sir', said Mrs Flittersnoop, and she went into the kitchen to finish reading her book.

The clock on the mantelpiece said four o'clock as the Professor fastened the safety pins that he had on his coat because the buttons had fallen off, and sat down to write.

He wrote to his auntie and his cousin and his special friend. He wrote to the butcher by mistake about some cabbages, and he wrote to the Mayor about a nasty smell that seemed as if it might be drains but was really a disused bone that Mrs

Flittersnoop's sister's dog had pushed under the carpet. Then he wrote to the BBC to say that someone was making squeaky noises on the wireless and to the laundry to say would they send back two buttonholes that were missing from his blue shirt.

'Only half-past four,' he said, looking at the clock. He had another half-hour to write letters and he'd written all his letters, so he thought for a bit and then wrote some postcards.

He wrote one to the water company to say that the water came out of the taps twisted, and was this all right? He wrote one to the coal people to say that the coal they sent was all dirty. He sent a picture postcard of himself to his friend Colonel Dedshott of the Catapult Cavaliers, saying he could come to tea on Sunday, and he sent one of Colonel Dedshott to himself to remind him that he was coming and another to Mrs Flittersnoop to remind her to get some crumpets because the Colonel liked them.

Then he looked at the clock and it was still half-past four.

'Well, I must have written those postcards quickly,' he said, looking at the clock through his long-sighted spectacles, and he was just wondering what to write next when Mrs Flittersnoop tapped at the door and came in with a cup of tea and a nice big piece of coconut cake.

'Please, sir, it's gone nine o'clock, and it's your bath night,' she said.

'Don't be silly,' said the Professor, stirring his tea and fishing out his near-sighted glasses that had fallen in. 'Look at the clock, it's half-past four. It's been half-past four for quite a long time.'

'There now,' said Mrs Flittersnoop, 'if the clock hasn't stopped.'

'Well, if it hasn't stopped what has it done?' said the Professor, deciding not to have his bath after all, as it was so late. 'There must be something wrong with it,' he went on, forgetting to put sugar in his tea and wishing he'd remembered. 'I'll take it down to the clock-man when I go out to the post.'

'I'll wrap it up for you, sir,' said Mrs Flittersnoop, and she took the clock out, leaving a dusty patch on the mantelpiece where it had stood.

Presently the Professor finished his tea and went out into the kitchen to get the clock.

'What a nice tidy packet,' he said, picking up the parcel from the kitchen-table, and he was gone before Mrs Flittersnoop, who was in the middle of a chapter, could tear herself away and tell him he'd taken a bag of potatoes by mistake and that the clock was on the hall-stand.

When he got to the clock-man's shop it was shut, but the clock-man knew him, so he let him in.

'Please, this clock has stopped,' said the Professor. He put down the parcel, cut the string, and all the potatoes burst out, rolled across the counter and went bouncing and bobbing all over the floor.

'Dear me,' said the Professor, wondering whether clocks always turned into potatoes when they stopped and that, if so, how awkward it was.

'Seventeen little ones and six big ones,' said the clock-man, who had been crawling round the shop picking up the potatoes. 'Twenty-three all told. Is that all?'

'I think there was another one,' said the Professor, who thought you bought potatoes in dozens. But there wasn't another one, so they didn't find it, even though they both looked through all five pairs of the Professor's spectacles one after the other.

'I'd better come back in the morning,' said the Professor, so the clock-man went to bed and the Professor went back with the potatoes and dropped absolutely several of them on the way.

Next day he took the stopped clock to the clock-man, who looked at it through a little spy glass, tapped it and turned it upside down, listened to it, smelt it, scratched about inside it with a hairpin and warmed it over the gas.

- WARMED IT OVER
THE GAS -

'It wants winding up,' he said. 'That's why it stopped, and that will be fivepence-halfpenny.'

But the Professor hadn't listened to him any further than 'It wants winding up.' He was scratching his head with one finger and saying to himself: 'Wants winding up. Now why should it want winding up? Because it has run down. What one wants is a clock that doesn't run down and therefore doesn't have to be wound up. Someone ought to invent a clock like that. Invent . . . Ha! Who invents things? Professors do, of course, and aren't I a professor? Yes, I am, so I'll invent a clock that doesn't need winding up,' and he was just going to rush out when the clock-man caught him by the coat-tails.

'Here,' he said, 'while you're about it you might invent one of those clocks that don't run down for *me*, will you, and we'll say no more about the fivepence-halfpenny.'

So the Professor said all right, he would invent two clocks, one for himself and one for the clock-man, and he went off to invent them, saying no more about the fivepence-halfpenny.

It didn't take the Professor as long to invent the clocks as he thought it was going to. In fact, it would have taken him less time still, only he found he'd run out of little weeny screws and had to send Mrs Flittersnoop out to buy a pennyworth.

On Sunday when Colonel Dedshott came to tea both the clocks were ready, even though he came immediately after breakfast. The Colonel always came to tea early, so as not to be late.

'And you mean to say those clocks will keep on going and telling the time right without ever being wound up,' said the Colonel, and he listened patiently while the Professor explained in awfully complicated language just how they worked. But he didn't understand a bit how they worked when the Professor had finished. He never could understand the Professor's inventions. They made his head go round and round so.

- THE PROFESSOR EXPLAINED -

'Now we'll take one of the clocks down to the clock-man I promised it to,' said the Professor, putting on his golfing cap which he always wore on Sunday to save his proper week-day hat.

'Hurray,' said the clock-man when he saw it. 'Thanks ever so, but I bet it runs down and has to be wound, all the same.'

'No, it won't,' said the Professor, 'not if you don't touch it. You see.'

So the clock-man said he'd see and he put it on the mantelpiece in his best parlour, taking away the dish of stuffed bananas that he used to keep there and putting them under the bath.

'Ta, ta,' said the Professor.

He raised his cap and all his spectacles fell off, but luckily none of them broke. The Colonel picked them up for him, saluted, clicked his heels and kissed his hand, and back they went, leaving the clock-man all excited to see if the clock would really go without winding.

The Professor and the Colonel were just having dinner together and the Professor was asking the Colonel to have a little more of everything to finish his lovely bread, when something happened.

The Professor's beautiful, marvellous and amazing never-stop clock went and struck thirteen!

'Coo,' said the Colonel with his mouth full, quite forgetting his manners he was so astonished. 'Is it meant to do that or has it got a pain in its cogwheels?'

'I shouldn't worry, sir, if I was you,' put in Mrs Flittersnoop, who had come in with a rice pudding. 'Clocks is funny things. I remember my sister Aggie had one that wouldn't go unless it was on its face, and then when it struck thirteen and the hands said a quarter to three you knew it was five o'clock.'

But the Professor was awfully upset. He wouldn't finish his dinner and he walked up and down the room till he nearly wore the carpet out.

'Oh dear, let's run down to the clock-man and see

if his clock has struck thirteen too,' he said at last, and he dashed out of the house without waiting to put his hat on or even to take his napkin out of his collar where he always tucked it in at meal-times.

When they got to the clock-man's he was all bothered and astonished too, because his clock had just struck fourteen.

'I see what I've done, yes I do,' shouted the Professor, while the clock-man was waving his arms and telling the Colonel that what he didn't know about clocks wasn't worth knowing, and that fourteen was a silly time for any clock to strike.

'I forgot all about the striking business,' went on the Professor, taking no notice of either of them. 'I've made the clocks so's they'll go for ever and never need winding and, of course, I've made them so's they go on striking for ever and not need winding. Only I forgot to put a little wiggly thing in, and instead of starting to strike one again after they've struck twelve, those clocks will go on striking thirteen, fourteen, fifteen and so on till they're striking goodness knows how many. Oh, dear,' and he sank wearily into a chair; only the Colonel had just taken the chair to sit on, so he sat bump on the floor instead.

'But listen, this is awful,' he went on, getting all worked up but forgetting to get up. 'The clocks'll go on striking fifteen, sixteen, seventeen, eighteen, on and on.'

'And every hour they'll strike more and more,' put in the clock-man, just to show he knew all about clocks.

'And soon they'll be striking so many strikes that

they won't have time to finish striking one hour before it's time to begin striking the next. And what's going to happen then? Oh dear,' cried the Professor. 'Oh, I must do something to the clock I've got, somehow, I must,' and getting up, he rushed back to his house again with the Colonel trying to keep up with him and the clock-man calling after him to hurry up and come back and do something to his clock, too.

When they got back there was a letter from the water company to say they didn't mind the water coming out twisted, but that if it came out in knots, to let them know. But the Professor didn't stop to read it. He dashed out into his inventory and came back with an armful of tools. Then he started trying to get the clock open.

He tried the screwdriver and the saw and he tried chisels, and he tried the tin-opener, but none of them was any good. Then he tried lots of tools of his own invention, but they weren't any good, either. For days and days he tried, and Mrs Flittersnoop got tired of waiting dinner for him and went to stay with her sister Aggie for a bit. Then the clock struck eighty-five, and in despair the Professor started biting it. But that wasn't any good either, and before long the never-stop clock was going *dong, dong, dong, dong, dong*, all the time without a pause.

'Oh dear, I'll never invent a clock again, no I won't,' gasped the Professor, now all tired out and weary.

Then there came a knock at the door, and the clock-man's little girl came in to say that father said their clock was humming.

'Humming,' said the Professor. 'Clocks don't hum. But, oh yes, of course. It's striking so many that it hasn't time to catch itself up and it has to keep on striking quicker and quicker, so it goes *dong-ng-ng* all the time.'

'Yes,' said the clock-man's little girl, 'that's just how it is going.'

'Go and tell your father to come and see me,' said the Professor, giving her a handful of nails in mistake for a handful of sweets. Then he went out into the garden to think.

But just as he was beginning to start getting ready to think there was a loud bang in the distance, and the next minute the clock-man dropped out of the sky right on to the calceolarias.

'Oh, you needn't have hurried so,' said the Professor, but the clock-man was waving his arms and trying to say everything at once. And his clothes were all torn and his face all dirty.

'The clock,' he managed to stammer out at last. 'It went bang. It started humming. It hummed and hummed and got shriller and shriller and then bang it went, and here I am.'

IT WENT BANG

'Good heavens!' cried the Professor, clutching at a hollyhock to steady himself. 'Of course, it kept striking quicker and quicker to catch itself up, and the quicker it struck the shriller it would make it hum, and . . .' He stopped suddenly, for from the house came a shrill wailing screech. *Weeeeeee!*

'The clock!' yelled the Professor. 'It's going to go bang, and my clock is a much bigger one than yours and if yours blew you all the way here, whatever will happen if my bigger clock goes bang?'

They dashed into the house. The Professor dashed to the mantelpice. He grabbed the screaming clock and dashed out of the window, forgetting to open it first and smashing the glass, *bing!*, all over the place.

Down the road he rushed, through Great Pagwell, past the ruins of the clock-man's house that his clock had blown up, and down to Lower Pagwell, with the clock shrieking and screeching and getting shriller at every stride. He passed Mrs Flittersnoop, who was on the way back to see if he was ready for dinner yet, but when she saw him and heard the clock, she went back to her sister Aggie's again.

Over the hedge dashed the Professor and down to the lake.

Screeeeech!, went the clock.

The Professor drew back his hand and hurled it as far as ever he could, which wasn't very far; then he turned and rushed back.

Boom, whoosh, ploshety, bing! The clock burst with a terrific crash and blew up so much water from the lake that everyone in Lower Pagwell got a bath although it wasn't bath night.

THE CLOCK BURST
WITH A TERRIFIC CRASH –

'I'm sorry about your house being all busted,' said the Professor to the clock-man, 'but I'll invent you a new one, shall I?'

But the clock-man said he'd rather invent his own house, thank you all the same.

From *The Incredible Adventures of Professor Branestawm*

Branestawm's
Crazy Clock

Unlike Professor Branestawm's screaming clocks, most ordinary clocks tell you what time it is, unless you've forgotten to wind them or taken them to bits to invent them into other things, as the Professor does. But Professor Branestawm's crazy clock tells you what time you want it to be, which is more encouraging.

To make it, you need a disc of cardboard about 24 cm in diameter, marked out with the numbers of a clock face. This is quite easy. Draw a circle with compasses set at 12 cm radius. Place the point of the compasses on the circumference (outside edge) of the circle, and mark off the circumference into equal sections, using the same 12 cm radius. It will divide into six parts. Now divide each of these in halves and you have the twelve divisions for the numbers of the clock face. To make it easier to draw the numbers properly, so that they radiate from the centre, draw fine pencil lines from each of the twelve divisions to the centre of the circle. Now draw the numbers with a nice, thick, felt-tipped pen, moving the circle round so that all the numbers face the centre. This way the number 6 will be upside-down when the clock face is held with the number 12 at the top.

With the compasses in the centre of the dial, draw a little circle about 2 or 3 cm in diameter in the centre of the dial. You have already drawn faint lines from the twelve divisions on the outer edge of the circle to the centre. These divide the little circle into twelve parts. Make a hole with a bradawl or the point of your compasses at each of these divisions, so that you have a little circle of holes in the centre of the dial. Number these holes, on the back of the dial, to correspond with the big numbers on the front of the dial. See Figure 1.

So that this circle of holes shan't be noticed and make awkward people start thinking it has something to do with the working of the clock (which it has), you should decorate the clock face with more holes. A good way to do this is to draw a design on the clock face with the compasses. Set the compasses to the radius of the clock as before. Put the point of the compasses to the radius to of the clock as before. Put the point of the compasses on the point you marked on the outer edge of the clock at the position 12. Scribe a line right across the clock face. Do the same with the point of the compasses at 2, 4, 6, 8 and 10. This will give you six leaf-shaped designs on the clock face. Using the point of the compass, prick

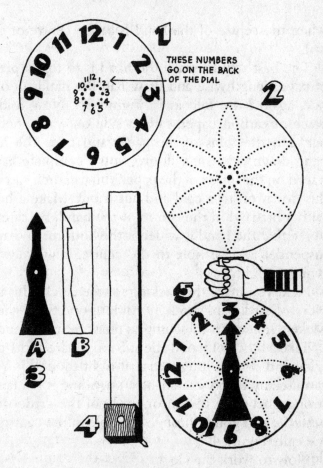

THESE NUMBERS GO ON THE BACK OF THE DIAL

holes at regular intervals along the leaves. See Figure 2.

Next you want a hand for the clock. This clock has only one hand because it tells only the hours, minutes being a bit too small for it to bother with. Cut a hand out of cardboard as shown in Figure 3. The hand should be just long enough for the tip of the point to come at the bottom of the numbers when the centre of the hand is at the centre of the dial.

The best way to make the hand is to fold a piece of paper lengthwise and draw half the hand on one side, against the fold as in Figure 3B. Now fold a piece of carbon paper, carbon side outwards, put it between the folds of the paper and trace the half hand down, when it will give you a complete hand traced on the inside of the paper. You can then carbon this down on to a card and cut it out. Make a hole with a bradawl in the centre of the hand. Be careful to see that the hand is wider at the bottom, so that if suspended by the hole in the centre, it will always swing upright.

Next you make the backing for the clock. This is a piece of cardboard about 35 cm long and 5 cm wide. Make a hole with the compass point near one end.

Take a block of wood about 5 cm square and 1 cm wide and drive a long thin nail right though it. You can use any empty match-box, providing it is a fairly strong one. Glue this to one side of the cardboard, with the nail going through the hole in the centre of the card. Figure 4.

Now to work the clock.

Suppose you want the time to be three o'clock. Take the dial and fit it on the backboard by pushing the hole in the little centre circle opposite the number 3 over the projecting nail in the backboard. Hold the dial against the backboard with the number 12 at the top and put the hand on the clock, the nail going through the hole in the middle of the hand.

Now give the hand a spin and release the dial but

hold on to the backboard, of course, or otherwise the whole lot will fall on the floor.

As the hand spins you will find the dial will move slowly round and when the hand stops the number 3 will be at the top of the dial and the hand will come to rest pointing to it. Figure 5.

You can make the clock stop at any hour simply by putting the dial on the backboard with the nail through the hole in the little circle that is opposite the number you want.

Be careful to make the holes in the dial and hand big enough for them to rotate freely on the nail, and don't push the dial or the hand hard against the backboard. Leave them free enough to turn.

Now how about setting Branestawm's crazy clock to tea-time and having a lovely nosh-up?

From *Professor Branestawm's Do-It-Yourself Handbook*

The
Expandable House

Colonel Dedshott of the Catapult Cavaliers was having a nice luxurious after-dinner look at his picture postcards of famous regiments when Professor Branestawm burst in with pairs of spectacles seeming to be falling off every part of him as he waved a roll of paper in his hand and scattered picture postcards of Generals and Corporals and Demi-Sergeants most indiscriminately all over the place.

'Amazing discovery that will astonish the world, Dedshott,' cried the Professor, flinging open the large roll of paper, which came apart into dozens of little rolls, and a stale bun with a bite out which the Professor had forgotten to go on with. 'Greatest invention of our time. It will change all our ideas of, er, that is, it will, er, ah.'

'Pah!' snorted the Colonel, shutting his postcard album just too late to stop three Captains of

Mounted Signallers from sliding into the fender.

'Listen,' said the Professor, trying to keep a very rolled up roll of paper out flat with one hand and a photo of the Colonel's Cousin Helen. 'Houses are most unsatisfactory.'

'Most,' agreed the Colonel, who was always having to have things done to his after the Professor had been demonstrating his rather bustable inventions in it.

'Either', went on the Professor, 'they have not enough rooms for everyone likely to stay in them at one time, or if the number of rooms is sufficient adequately to accommodate the largest number of inhabitants, then it follows that when some of those inhabitants are, er, absent, the number of, ah, um, rooms becomes at once too great. You follow me, Dedshott?'

'Hm,' grunted the Colonel, still picking up postcards.

'I have invented a new kind of house which will do away with all that.' He swept his hand round and did away with four china vases. 'An expandable, adaptable, contractable, adjustable house, Dedshott. Made of an elastic material largely composed of rubber. Each room is fitted with a special valve and may be pumped up or let down according to the number of persons in the house.'

'Wonderful,' said the Colonel, feeling more at home now that his head was beginning to go round and round as it usually did when listening to the Professor describing inventions. 'Don't know how you think of these things, Branestawm. Jolly clever, what!'

'Er, not at all,' said the Professor. 'One has one's, um, ah, job to do, Dedshott. I have had constructed a specimen of my new type of adjustable house, and I was wondering if you would care to come and stay a few days in it with me. Just by way of an, ah, experiment.'

'Yes. Good idea,' said the Colonel, who had guessed something of the sort was coming, but hadn't been able to think of an excuse to get out of it, short of saying he was going to stay with his Cousin Helen, and was afraid the Professor would invite her too. And Cousin Helen in an adjustable house with let-downable rooms was unthinkable. She was so unadjustable herself, as you might say, being considerably on the large side.

The next day, the Colonel arrived on his best horse at the Professor's, and found Mrs Flittersnoop busily dusting the outside of what looked like an enormous bunch of grapes on the lawn.

'Ha, there you are, Dedshott,' said the Professor's voice, and the Professor himself burst silently out of a door in the bunch of grapes. 'Here you see my new adjustable house. The rooms are somewhat ball-shaped because it is so difficult to make anything blow-upable a square shape, owing to the corners becoming de-cornered in the inflating process.'

'Amazing,' said the Colonel, who wasn't listening much, as he didn't want his head to start going round, because his horse was already going round by itself, and he had all he could do to get off it at the right time and place.

'It is all very simple and convenient,' said the

Professor, showing the Colonel round his excessively round house. 'The motor which carries the house in its folded condition generates heat for cooking and light for, er, er . . .'

'Lightning,' said the Colonel, not seeing what else it could be for.

'Precisely, Dedshott. These' – the Professor pointed to a number of sticking-out parts, which made the bunch-of-grapes-looking house look as if the stalks were growing on the wrong end of the grapes – 'these are the pumping up and letting down valves. Supposing, for instance, that we do not require this particular bedroom. We simply unscrew the valve cap and *voilà!*'

It wasn't so much *voilà* as *we-e-e-e-e-e-p-zug*, as the not-wanted room went down like ten bicycle tyres with none too slow punctures, and the escaping air blew the Colonel's hat off in spite of it being held on with elastic; a military precaution against being de-hatted which he had learned from a picture postcard of a Mountain Musketeer.

'The rooms have double walls,' went on the Professor, taking no notice. 'The air is pumped between the thickness; but that is not all, Dedshott. My house, being made from a material largely composed of rubber in order to make it, er, stretchable, is also weatherproof. In the winter it prevents the warmth from getting out and in the summer it stops the heat from getting in. A most desirable arrangement.'

They went inside, and Mrs Flittersnoop served them a most appropriate dinner consisting of an omelette, which began by being enormously large but gradually shrank down to a very skinny fried-egg-looking one as it cooled. It was made from a recipe the Professor had invented, and it should have been fastened down with drawing-pins until needed.

At last it was bedtime.

'Here is your room, Dedshott,' said the Professor, pointing to something that looked like many mackintoshes in a mound.

'Allow me!' He pulled an elastic lever and *puff, puff, puff, woof,* the mackintosh-looking mound expanded into a bedroom all done out in pink pansies and with the Colonel's initials embroidered on the ceiling, which was a little surprise Mrs Flittersnoop had prepared.

Next morning the Colonel woke up in a bush.

'Pah!' he growled. 'Confound these invented sort of houses of Branestawm's. Something unusual gone wrong as usual I suppose.'

But actually, nothing had gone wrong and it wasn't the Professor's fault that he was so out in the open. The Colonel's horse, which he had tied to a disused croquet hoop, had got away and bitten off the valve arrangement of the 'Colonel's room, thinking it was some kind of a horsey sort of food. Then, of course, the Colonel's bedroom had gone very wizzily down, *z-z-z-z-z-z-m*. Goodness knows what would have happened to the Colonel. He might easily have been smothered with his own initials as the ceiling came down, but luckily for him he was no end of a one for fresh air, and he'd left his bedroom window wide open. So when the room went down, it simply squeezed him gently but firmly out of the window like so much toothpaste out of a tube.

Breakfast was only half over before the Professor began pulling elastic levers and twiddly adaptable valves. Air puffed in and zizzed out with noises ranging from that of ten impatient trains leaving Pagwell Junction in a bunch to that of one weary pussy-cat leaving some dinner he didn't care for. Finally the Professor let the whole house down into a fairly generous-sized heap of folded sort of flollops, rolled it into a motor van kindly lent by Mrs Flittersnoop's sister Aggie's Bert, who, as a rule, used it for carrying such things as coals or vegetables, or children to picnics, and was obliging the Professor for the day.

'Well, Branestawm, I must say you've excelled yourself this time. My word, yes, you know, what!' said the Colonel, deciding to say no more about being squeezed out of the window. 'Most clever idea. Highly useful for soldiers and all that, you know. Better than tents, handier than barracks and more comfortable than bivouacs, by Jove. My friend, the General, must see this, Branestawm.'

'Er, yes, yes, of course,' said the Professor. 'But the, er, fact is, Dedshott, I have already promised it in a way to the Pagwell Council, who are coming to see it tomorrow.'

'Pah!' snorted the Colonel, who didn't care much for the Pagwell Council as they kept making him pay rates for things he didn't agree with. 'I'll bring the General here tomorrow. Meet Pagwell Council, confound them, and we shall see, yes, by Jove, sir.' And with a flourishing salute to Mrs Flittersnoop, who nearly fell over a clothes-basket in trying to curtsey back again, the Colonel was gone.

Then the Professor got his house off Bert's van, pumped up the kitchen in mistake for a bedroom and went to sleep in the sink.

Professor Branestawm's expandable house was blown up to its uttermost utmost. The Mayor of Pagwell and several important members of the Council were being entertained to tea and house-blowing demonstrations. So was Colonel Dedshott's General and one or two of the General's Assistant-Generals and decorative Majors. Mrs Flittersnoop and her sister Aggie and sister Aggie's litle girl were serving tea, which they had made secretly behind a bush outside, as sister Aggie wasn't too sure if she agreed with collapsible kitchens.

'You see, gentlemen, my invention is all, and more, I, er, claim it to, um, ah, be,' said the Professor, looking round through all sorts of pairs of spectacles.

'Marvellous,' grunted Colonel Dedshott, taking another piece of seed cake as the General had been eating off his plate by mistake.

It was a severely separated and definitely disconnected kind of tea party. Because no one room of the house would hold all the imposing people at one go. So some of them were in the dining-room, some in the lounge. Colonel Dedshott, his General, and his General's friends sat in neat military rows in various bedrooms. The Mayor of Pagwell sat in state in the bath, propped up with cushions. And the Professor,

who had left all the doors open to make polite conversation easy, if none too simple, owing to talking round corners so to speak, sat nowhere at all, but ran about spilling tea into umbrella stands.

'Certainly, certainly,' said the General, passing the Colonel's cup for more tea and taking a bite out of a tart belonging to a Major. 'Say no more about it, Professor. We approve the idea entirely. Yes, indeed. Just what the Army wants, sir. Every man carries his own house. Movable barracks, my word. What do you say, Dedshott?'

'Marvellous,' agreed the Colonel, picking up the General's cup, but the General had already emptied it.

'What about drains?' asked the Pagwell Councillor who saw to inspecting sanitary sorts of things.

'Negotiations for securing the proposition will commence forthwith,' said the General, borrowing an Assistant-General's pencil.

'Wait a minute there, not so fast,' said the Pagwell Councillor in charge of streets and houses. 'This is not a military idea at all, sir. I want streets of these houses laid out in Pagwell for the winter, then in summer, as people go for holidays, the houses can be de—, er, de—, er, let down, folded up and deposited at the Town Hall until required.'

'Thus leaving additional space for recreation grounds and playing fields,' put in the Pagwell Councillor who looked after sports and pastimes.

'Nation's defence comes before nation's convenience, sir!' shouted the General, leaning forward to talk round into the dining-room, which didn't help, as the Councillors were on the piano in the drawing-room. 'Have the kindness to withdraw, sir.'

'What about drains?' said the Sanitary Councillor again.

'Another cup of tea, sir?' said Mrs Flittersnoop, taking his cup and handing it to sister Aggie, who poured out no end of hot water, as she'd forgotten to put tea in the pot.

'No, er, drains are necessary, I assure you,' said the Professor, 'though it would, I fear, take rather long to, ah, explain why.'

'Hear, hear,' said a Pagwell Councillor, whose own drains had gone wrong at home.

'Confound it, sir, this is no mere matter of drains!' shouted the General. 'Safety of nation may be at stake. Do you hear, sir? Safety of nation. And you talk about drains. Pah! Yes, sir, pah!'

'Perhaps we had, er, better see what the, ah, Mayor has to say,' suggested the Professor, blinking about a bit as things began to get arguish.

But the Mayor had gone to sleep in the bath and was dreaming that the rates had gone up to double.

The arguments grew fiercer and noisier. The house swayed with the thumping of fists and bouncing of bodies inside it. Suddenly Mrs Flittersnoop gave a shriek.

'Oh my goodness, sir, indeed. Look, sir, look if we aren't blowing away, sir, oh dear, dear!' she screamed.

The Professor looked out of a window. Oo-er! The blow-upable house had broken from its foundations owing to the bashing about inside. The wind had caught it and was blowing it up in a way the Professor had never intended. A queer balloon, sailing high above the tree-tops.

That stopped the argument. Partly because the General didn't want soldiers who might go up in the air at a moment's notice, partly because the Streets and Houses Councillor didn't want houses that might run away with people before the rent could be collected. But most of all because they were all too scared about being up in the air to do any more arguing.

'Keep calm, keep calm,' said the Professor, getting frightfully flurried. 'I will open some of the valves and we shall descend gently.'

'No, no!' cried Colonel Dedshott, who had no wish to be squeezed toothpaste fashion out of windows hundreds of feet up in the air. 'Rooms will collapse, by Jove, yes, sir. Pull levers, Branestawm. Twiddle those wheel things. Confound it, sir, pull levers, pull levers!'

But, alas! Lever pulling was no use this time. No! It was a case of open valves and be squeezed out high above the tree-tops or leave them closed and be blown goodness knows where.

Suddenly, there was the most exaggeratedly explosive kind of pop, like three hundred pounds' worth of penny balloons being busted at once. The next second the Professor's house was in bits of various sizes which were flying off at various angles, while the Professor, the Colonel, the Councillors, Generals, and Mayor were falling in a heap with the wind whistling past their eyebrows.

Sister Aggie's little girl had done it. Yes, she had.

She'd tried to fix a calendar on the expandable kitchen wall with a pin. A pin, mind you, in a blow-up inflatable house. Oo-er! No wonder the bang and the bits!

Down they shot, and whizzed, and whistled, and dropped. Pagwell canal glinted beneath them like a silver ribbon with tucks in it. Very pretty! But who notices pretty things when they're falling into them? Down, down, down! But ha! Thank goodness a barge happened to be passing along the canal. And the barge was full of straw being delivered to the Camels Back Brick Factory. They landed with a series of soft plonks into the straw. Very undignified, but not more so than landing in the water, and ever so much drier. But the Mayor was missing from the straw-landers. A little way off, though, there was a noticeable splash; the Mayor had landed in the canal. He was in the bath, but no longer asleep. The bath acted as a boat. Luckily the plug was in and kept the water out instead of keeping it in as bath plugs usually do.

The Mayor seized a back-scrubbing brush and paddled himself along. And he enjoyed it so much that they had rather a job to get him to come out.

And that was almost the end of the Professor's expandable house. But not quite. For the pieces were picked up in various places by various people who used them as make-do mackintoshes and temporary umbrellas and meantime sponge bags, according to what sort of people they were; while the Professor brought his idea down a bit small and made an expandable meat-safe which could be blown up on Saturday, ready for Sunday's joint, and gradually let down as the week passed through the stages of cold joint, warmed-up joint, stew, hash, soup and cat's dinner. But, of course, one had to be careful of skewers.

From *Professor Branestawm's Treasure Hunt*

Professor Branestawm's Dictionary Quiz

Words are strange things. Playing with them can be fun, but you have to be careful. Some of the very long, curly ones are apt to wind themselves round you and dislocate your pronunciation. And some words don't mean what they look or sound as if they ought to mean. Take the word 'inventory', for instance. If you pronouce it '*inv*' nt'ry, as you are supposed to, it means a list of things. But if you pronounce it 'in*vent*ory', as the Professor does, then it means a place where you invent things.

Professor Branestawm felt it was time some kind of research was done into words like these, so he invented a completely new kind of dictionary (or *fictionary*, as he calls it), especially for all those words that seem to have better meanings than the ones usually given to them. These are some of the entries that appear in the Professor's dictionary – see if you can match up words with their definitions.

1. A convenient hat
2. A thing for starting a motor car
3. The lower part of the lady's face
4. A waltz for cakes
5. A frog too tired to leap
6. What policemen get paid for working overtime in the evening
7. A fine for naughtiness
8. An Eskimo's toilet
9. A container for a bossy person
10. Change the colour of a piece of wood

A. Bulletin
B. Igloo
C. Khaki
D. Out-of-bounds
E. Syntax
F. Abundance
G. Dialogue
H. Urchin
I. Handicap
J. Copper Nitrate

Answers on page 188

From *Professor Branestawm's Dictionary*

The Professor Stays
with Sister Aggie

Of course, Mrs Flittersnoop frequently went to stay with her sister Aggie, in Lower Pagwell. She went whenever the Professor's inventions rather busted the place up, which was none too seldom.

But this time, what with a special oil stove the Professor had invented setting fire to his house while he was out, and on top of that, his too conscientious wireless fire alarms getting the Pagwell Fire Brigade all muddled up, the Professor's house was more than usually drastically done for and not liveable-in. So the Professor had gone with Mrs Flittersnoop to stay with sister Aggie.

'Come along in, sir, I'm only too pleased to have you,' said Aggie. And in the Professor was hustled, fussed around, clothes brushed, spectacles arranged in the wrong order and sat in an armchair that was considerably more comfortable than it looked. Then

129

Mrs Flittersnoop and sister Aggie disappeared into the kitchen and there began the noises of cups of things being got ready, and plenty of arranging sort to talk, so as to give the Professor the best bedroom, which looked out on Lower Pagwell High Street, with trams going slowly and clankily by very frequently when you wanted to get to sleep, but very rarely when you were waiting for one.

Next morning the Professor was awakened at half-past five by sister Aggie's husband, who drove one of the better-class trams, going out by the back door so as not to spoil the front step. And later on by the sound of sister Aggie's little girl being got ready for school, which seemed to take plenty of time, and which sounded rather like lots and lots of children being got ready to go to the seaside for a fortnight.

'Um!' said the Professor, picking his five pairs of spectacles carefully off the brass bed-rail where he'd hung them the night before so as to be tidy in someone else's house.

He was just going to start marking out an invention on the wallpaper when there came a tap on the door and sister Aggie brought in a cup of tea.

'I didn't bring it before so as not to disturb you,' she beamed. She let up the blinds with a crash. 'I always think it is nice to have a bit of a sleep in the first morning in a strange bed.'

When she had gone the Professor stacked his spectacles carefully on his nose, and sipped his tea. But oh dear! Sister Aggie was so hasty and hearty in her way of doing things she'd slopped positively quantities of the tea in the saucer. And it dropped off the bottom of the cup, right splash on the best counterpane that sister Aggie's grandma had embroidered with her own hands.

'Tut, tut, most careless of me,' muttered the Professor, thinking the mess was his fault, which it wasn't for a change. 'Dear, dear, what will Mrs, er, Aggie think of me?' He put the cup and saucer down beside him and began very earnestly rubbing at the tea-stained counterpane with the sleeve of his pyjamas. This made very little difference to the stain, but knocked over the cup of tea, *slosh!*, all over the best pillow with lace trimming made by sister Aggie's cousin Mabel's own hands.

'Oh! my goodness. How very careless of me,' wailed the Professor. 'I, er, really, er, this is most, er . . . It places me in a most awkward position.'

Thank goodness Mrs Flittersnoop took it into her head to come up with another cup of tea very neatly set out on a small, round tray with a paper what's-its-name under it, and not a spot spilled. Knowing what her sister Aggie was with cups of things.

Shattering noises were coming from the bicycle shed sister Aggie had let Professor Branestawm use as a make-do inventory. It contained no bicycles, but it was considerably stacked up with portions of old mangle, spare bits of old pram, finished-with kettles, collapsed sewing machines, once-new wheelbarrows and other drastically dealt with domestic machinery.

Professor Branestawm didn't mind. He liked to have plenty of odd cog-wheels about. He was never really happy without quantities of disjointed works.

He thoroughly enjoyed a few unintentional spokes.

He was inventing a special unsloppable cup and saucer, particularly for the benefit of sister Aggie and other hearty but none too steady-handed people.

'Liquid will always find its own level,' said the Professor, remembering something he had learned at school. 'But the question is this. Is the level that belongs to tea the same level as that which is the property of cocoa? And if so, how do they manage about it when they both find it together? Hum! Perhaps that may account in some way for the extreme sloppability of some liquids.'

The Professor put a pair of pliers on his nose in mistake for one of his pairs of spectacles and began again at the beginning.

He invented seven different sorts of cups that wouldn't slop blancmange, or treacle, or stiff honey. But they all positively did slop anything more runny if handled carelessly. He tried making them different shapes, which caused them to look most rum and unteacup-like, but made them no less spillable.

At last the Professor lost his temper.

'Ridiculous!' he cried. 'Here am I, Theophilus Branestawm, inventor, master of mechanics, doctor of dynamics, and goodness knows what, unable to invent a merely special teacup. Pah! I never heard of such a thing. Didn't I invent a special spring-cleaning machine?' (My word he did.) 'Didn't I invent a never-stop clock, even though it did burst? Wasn't I responsible, through my pancake-making machine, for there being round paving-stones instead of square ones in Pagwell? What about Branestawm's non-shine glass, and Branestawm's burglar-catcher, and Branestawm's – pah! What are mere teacups?' The Professor certainly was annoyed. Just to show himself what was what, he invented a reversible mangle with shirt-shining attachment; a thing for getting the pips out of, and the skin off, grapes, while still leaving some grape. An automatic egg skinner, and an elastically driven brace-button replacer.

'Now!' he grunted. 'What about the unspillable teacup?' Either the Professor's rapid bit of inventing had sort of warmed up his brains, or else the idea he was waiting for was waiting for him, and got impatient. Anyway, all of a sudden, *voilà*. There was the perfect, unspillable teacup. In three designs (all of them awful, but never mind).

'Mrs Flittersnoop,' he cried, dashing out with the cups and arriving in the coal cellar instead of the kitchen because he'd forgotten it was sister Aggie's house he was at.

He filled the unspillable cups with tea specially made for the occasion, and Mrs Flittersnoop, sister Aggie and sister Aggie's little girl had a go at trying to slop the tea out of them.

They couldn't do it. They ran carelessly upstairs. They shot even more carelessly downstairs. They tripped over the mat, both intentionally and otherwise. They slipped down the banisters. But not one quarter of a drop of tea did they mange to spill.

'Very good, I'm sure, sir,' said Mrs Flittersnoop, and sister Aggie said, 'What will they think of next?'

'We must celebrate,' said the Professor. He dashed off with the still unspilled cups to make an enormous unspillable tea service, and to send invitations for a tremendous tea party.

Professor Branestawm's tea party in Pagwell Town Hall was to be a very ladylike, balance your cup on one knee sort of drawing-room kind of tea, because the Vicar's wife had kindly offered to help with the arrangements, and she was rather a one for being polite. Otherwise, Mrs Flittersnoop would have had what she called a good, sensible, sit-down meal, which meant you could eat more without appearing rude. Tea was being served from a long table full of the Professor's unspillable cups and a number of plates of rather pale, home-made gingerbread, kindly given by sister Aggie, who wasn't as good at ginger-bread as she thought she was. On the platform at the end of the hall, at a table with bigger cups and thinner gingerbread, sat the Mayor of Pagwell, who was going to make a speech if he got half a chance; Professor Branestawm, because it was his party; Colonel Dedshott, in case the Professor needed a bit of backing-up; the Vicar of Pagwell, because his wife had done some of the arranging; and Mr Bakewell Skoneligh, of the Pagwell Bakeries, because he had sent the tea-making apparatus and wanted to keep an eye on it.

Mrs Flittersnoop and sister Aggie poured out the tea into the Professor's unspillable cups, and everyone stood about waiting for someone to start first.

'Hum, er, ah, hum!' said the Professor, wondering if he ought to say something. But the Mayor and the Vicar both stood up together and said, 'Ladies and

Gentlemen,' then they looked at each other and sat down again, the Vicar on a piece of gingerbread the Professor had absently put on his chair. So the Mayor, who hadn't sat on any gingerbread, took advantage of his advantage, so to speak, and spoke.

'Ladies and Gentlemen,' he said, 'it gives me great pleasuah to be here today, on this notable and, perhaps I may say, auspicious occasion.'

'Bravo!' said Colonel Dedshott, and everyone applauded.

'To drink the first drop as it were', went on the Mayor, 'from Professor Branestawm's un—, er, un—, un—' 'Spillable,' murmured the Professor. 'Teacups,' finished the Mayor.

There was more applause, while the Mayor lifted his cup to his mouth very correctly, little finger sticking out and all. Presently he put it down again and there was a slight look of surprise on his face. He looked at the Professor, who was looking at a Town Hall spider on the ceiling, and didn't see him. He lifted his cup again and appeared to be trying, in as polite a way as possible, to eat it.

The Vicar lifted his cup. And his little finger stuck out even further than the Mayor's because he was even more used to polite tea parties.

Everyone else lifted their cups. Little fingers stuck out all over the place. The Professor beamed on everyone and forgot about his own cup of tea.

'How nice to have an invention that gives no trouble,' he thought. 'Nothing can go wrong this time. There are no cog-wheels that I might have missed out. No levers to get pulled the wrong way.

No super-differentials to slip . . . Good gracious!'

Good gracious it certainly was. The polite tea party was going through the most unusual convulsions. Everyone seemed to be trying to get inside his teacup. Necks wriggled. Eyes bulged. Heads waggled.

Oh, Professor Branestawm! Oh, those unspillable cups! Unspillable they certainly were. The Professor had made them unspillable by having a sort of turned-in lip round the edge, and so as to make absolutely, unspillably sure, he'd put a fairly generous lip round. Alas! The result was that although not a drop could possibly be spilt from the cups, neither could a drop possibly be drunk from them.

The Vicar had another piece of gingerbread and hoped for the best. Colonel Dedshott frowned into his cup and wondered if smashing it would be any use. The Mayor of Pagwell kept smiling vacantly and raising and lowering his cup, trying to pretend everything was quite all right.

'The principle on which these, er, cups are constructed,' said the Professor, thinking perhaps he might make everyone forget about their tea if he talked sufficient complications at them.

At that moment, little Willie Wibbelspeck, cousin of Mr Bakewell Skoneligh, the baker, fished out of his pocket a rather bent drinking straw, stuck one end in his unspillable cup of undrinkable tea and drank it up, rather impolitely, but completely successfully.

'Ha!' cried Colonel Dedshott. He had a few rapid whispery words with Mr Bakewell Skoneligh who vanished out of a side door while the Colonel got up and said, 'Er, ha, what! This reminds me of an experience I had when I was in the tropics, by Jove, yes.' And he began to tell them a very long-drawn-out, military kind of un-joke about mosquitoes, but, fortunately, he was only about two-thirds through it when the baker returned with an armful of drinking straws which he managed to get hurriedly passed round. So the party managed to finish up drinking rather cold sort of tea through straws, which was all right except when a tea leaf stuck in a straw, which it frequently did.

'Well! Never mind, sir, it was very clever, I'm sure,' said Mrs Flittersnoop afterwards. And the Professor didn't mind so much because he'd just heard that his own house would be ready to move back to on Friday.

Next morning, sister Aggie brought him up a cup of tea as usual, in an ordinary cup, with exactly three-sevenths of it slopped in the saucer. So the Professor poured the rest out of the cup and drank it all out of the saucer, with no finger sticking out and the trams clattering past as loudly as ever.

From *Professor Branestawm's Treasure Hunt*

Friendly and
Unfriendly Needles

D o needles like each other or don't they? That is one of the world-shaking questions Professor Branestawm has been investigating. And he found that they do and they don't, so needles aren't so different from people, are they?

To demonstrate the Professor's sensational discovery you want two thick darning needles or bodkins. They must be both the same size and thickness. Stroke each one plenty of times with a magnet, starting at the eye and finishing at the point.

Now, on a level, smooth surface such as a piece of cardboard, place the needles side by side a little way apart with the eye of one needle opposite to the point of the other. Move the needles a little closer and you will find they jump together and cling like long lost friends. So that proves needles like each other.

But now separate the needles and lay them side by side, eyes together. You will find they refuse to stay next to each other and no matter how often you put them together they will move apart. So that proves needles don't like each other.

Perhaps that's what makes sewing so difficult.

From *Professor Branestawm's Do-It-Yourself Handbook*

The Professor Deals with Inflation

*S*queak, squeak, squeak, puff, puff, squeak. Was it mice nibbling at the foundations of the Town Hall? Could it be a new invention of Professor Branestawm's that needed oiling? No, it was the Vicar of Great Pagwell pumping up his bicycle tyres ready to visit deserving people.

'Ha, Vicar!' cried Commander Hardaport (Retired), rolling up with a telescope under one arm and the *Yachting World* under the other. 'Getting inflation under control, I see, ha ha ha!'

'Dear me, I wish I could,' murmured the Vicar, putting his pump back on his bicycle upside down. 'Things are getting most serious, you know, Commander, most serious.' He said it twice because he felt it sounded more serious that way. 'Everything is costing so much.'

'Ha, yes,' grunted the Commander, opening his

telescope and looking at a little bird on a tree, which resented it and flew away. 'The rates are too high for a start. Shan't pay 'em. And then there are the dustmen coming only once a fortnight. Don't know what to do with all the rubbish. Better give it to the *Pagwell Gazette* – they can print it with the other stuff.'

'I think we should form a deputation and see the Council about it,' said the Vicar, wishing he could charge for seats in church to get money to have the organ seen to.

'My word, yes,' shouted the Commander. 'Get Colonel Dedshott along, and Professor Branestawm. Make 'em listen, by jingo! Clear decks for action.'

Colonel Dedshott was only too ready for action, whether any decks were cleared for it or not. And as for Professor Branestawm, he immediately had fifteen ideas for beating inflation, some of which would have abolished rates, some of which would have abolished the Council and some of which could easily have abolished Pagwell itself.

Meantime Pagwell Council were already having an emergency meeting on very economy lines to decide what to do about inflation and high prices. They held it in the basement instead of in the Council Chamber because it felt more economical. All the Councillors wore old clothes so as to look as if they weren't spending any money and they had their morning tea half an hour late with not enough sugar in it.

'Hrmp!' said the Mayor. 'I think we should start with economies in the Council. It will set a good example, you know.'

'Hear, hear!' cried the Councillors, who were all for setting good example as long as they didn't have to follow them.

'I suggest that in future the Council's proceedings are recorded on the backs of old envelopes instead of in that expensive leather-bound book,' said the Mayor.

'And don't let's call them minutes,' said the Drains Councillor. 'Make it seconds, that's a lot less.'

'No, no, no!' cried the Treasurer. 'What we want is not so much ways of *saving* money as ways of getting more.'

'We can't put the rates up any higher,' protested the Parks and Gardens Councillor, who had already got into trouble for not paying his.

All these plans for beating inflation had progressed on a friendly basis for some time. Nobody had called anybody a rude name. Nobody had thrown anything and hardly anybody had shouted much above a whisper. But inflation was continuing all over the place and the Council decided to do something really drastic.

'We must reduce spending however much it costs,' cried the Town Clerk. 'And we must make more money however much we lose. I suggest we call in Professor Branestawm to help.'

But Professor Branestawm didn't need any calling in. He was already stamping round the Town Hall accompanied by the Vicar, Colonel Dedshott and Commander Hardaport (Retired) and an excitable door-keeper man who was trying to tell them they weren't allowed in. Eventually they tracked down the Councillors and the meeting blew up in table-thumpings and teeth-gnashings and highly inflammable language as the Professor and his friends told the Council what to do about things.

'I, er, um, ah,' said Professor Branestawm, after Commander Hardaport (Retired) had at last blown a fog horn he had brought with him to get some quiet. 'That is to say, what we need is some device which will make people want to pay money to the Council. Something that will cause them to, um, ah, rush along with money only too anxious to pay it.'

'Ha, ha ha! He he he! Ho ho ho!' laughed the Councillors, who thought that was a better joke than the ones on the telly.

'If we could do that we needn't have any rates,' said the Treasurer, shivering slightly at the thought of not having rates and having to do without those lovely final demand notices printed in red to look more alarming.

'Precisely!' said the Professor. 'It will make Pagwell the happiest town in the world.'

'What will?' asked the Drains Councillor, who had been asleep and had missed everything.

'Something to make the people come rushing here, gladly giving us money,' said the Mayor.

The Drains Councillor got so excited at hearing this that he nearly choked himself and somebody sent for a plumber to clear him.

'Nonsense!' roared the Councillor in charge of libraries, who was cross because his allowance for buying comics had been cut. 'The thing's impossible!

Nobody likes paying money to the Council. How are you going to get them to come rushing along to do it and like it?'

'Fun fair!' said Professor Branestawm, waving his five pairs of spectacles about. 'Dodgem cars, roundabouts, big dippers, haunted houses, water chutes...'

'Accompanied by military bands, by Jove!' put in Colonel Dedshott, who was determined that the Catapult Cavaliers should play their part.

'And miniature gunboats on the canal!' cried Commander Hardaport (Retired), banging the table with his telescope and upsetting the Mayor's tea. 'Naval displays! Sinking the submarine – sort of nautical coconut shy, ha ha!'

The Councillors opened their mouths and didn't say anything. They were speechless for the first time in living memory. They gave wonderful imitations of surprised goldfish. They flapped their hands like astonished seals. But at last they recovered long enough to instruct Professor Branestawm to proceed with all speed to create the Great Pagwell Fun Fair to cause people to come hurrying up with handfuls of lovely money, and then the meeting broke up without any confusion, except that all the Councillors' heads were going round and round even faster than Colonel Dedshott's.

Professor Branestawm's inventory buzzed and whizzed and hummed with activity. Coloured smoke and fancy stars emerged, and slight bangs exploded now and then. Mrs Flittersnoop got tired of trying to push cups of tea and sandwiches through the windows and asked the meals-on-Wheels people to deal with the Professor. But their dinners were only run over by some of his inventions, which turned then into wheels-on-meals.

Round about the time that the second final notices for paying the rates were due to go out, the Great Pagwell Municipal Fun Fair went into business. There was no opening ceremony in case people thought it was extravagant. The Mayor stayed at home, put on his robes and said, 'I declare the Fun Fair open,' to himself.

'Coo!' exclaimed the Great Pagwellians, when they saw the Fair, and rushed in with money at the ready, just as the Professor had said they would.

First of all, there were dodgem cars, specially contrived so that they went out of the Fun Fair and swept the streets. These not only saved Pagwell Council the cost of having the streets swept but also brought in money from people who paid to go in them.

'Of course people have to pay for having the streets swept,' said the Town Clerk. 'Only they prefer to pay for it by dodgem car rides and do it themselves, so everybody's happy.'

And happiest of all were the street-sweeping men who took over mowing the grass in the Pagwell Parks so that the mowing men could be released for other duties, and most of them were so old they preferred to stay at home and mow their own lawns.

Then there was an ingenious roundabout that worked the pumping station for the Pagwell water

supply. That saved no end of money because the pumping-station men were free to join the police, and criminals began to be caught three times as often, which was still hardly at all.

'Good old Branestawm, my word, what!' exclaimed Colonel Dedshott. He made a bonfire of all his rate demands and got fined half as much as the rates he didn't pay for emitting smoke in a smokeless zone.

The Fun Fair also included an ingenious game called 'Mending a Hole in the Road'. For this you paid your money and were given a little cart full of road-mending equipment and a map showing where all the holes were. You simply picked your hole, dashed off and filled it and came back. And if you filled your hole more quickly than anyone else had done you got your money back. But of course only one person could get his money back on that rule, so Pagwell Council made almost enough money to fill the holes in their budget.

Another Branestawm Fun Fair device was the 'Traffic Warden Game'. In this you paid for a warden's hat and a book of tickets, and then you went around the streets sticking tickets on all the cars that shouldn't be there. You got commission on the fines the owners had to pay, so that you made a nice profit. But some enthusiastic players stuck tickets on their own cars in the excitement and got fined more than they made. And one frightful player stuck a ticket on the car of the Head Policeman and was nearly sent to prison for a thousand years.

All these ingenious devices of Professor Branestawm's drew such a crowd and collected so much money that Pagwell Council were able not only to abolish rates altogether but actually to pay out pocket-money bonuses to the residents.

Nothing could possibly be more delightful. Pagwell became the most envied place in the country. Would-be emigrants from other places formed long snaky queues, hoping to find somewhere to live in Pagwell. Some people were willing even to move in to dog kennels but the dogs refused to move out.

'Marvellous, dear chap,' cried Commander Hardaport, slapping the Professor on the back.

'Most satisfactory,' purred the Vicar, who had been given a lovely lump of money by Pagwell Council to buy a new organ for the church.

'Yes, indeed, I'm sure, sir,' agreed Mrs Flittersnoop.

But a week later things began to happen.

The people who took out the dodgem cars found the streets were now so clean that there was nothing to sweep, and so they used the cars instead to go shopping. Then the Fun Fair traffic wardens gleefully swooped down and clapped tickets on them. But there was some argument as to whether a dodgem car was a ticketable vehicle within the meaning of the Act, and anyway the owners of the cars were Pagwell Council and they had to pay the fines themselves. The roundabouts were so busy and flew round at such a speed that water was pumped far too energetically and Pagwell householders got a bathful squirted over them every time they turned on a tap.

Then the mend-a-hole-in-the-road game made the roads so smooth and pleasant that traffic that didn't want to go anywhere near Pagwell went that way because it was such a beautiful ride. And the Pagwellians couldn't get out of their houses for the traffic congestion that was caused.

'This is terrible!' gasped the Town Clerk. 'Professor, you *must* do something about it. Your inventions! Your ideas! They have gone wrong as usual. Most inconvenient. Pagwell is in chaos.'

'Um, ah, pardon me,' said Professor Branestawm, arranging his spectacles firmly and going all indignant. 'My inventions have *not* gone wrong, they are working perfectly. It is your citizens who have gone wrong. If they choose to use my inventions in a way I did not intend that is not my, er, um, fault.' And he stalked away in a middle-sized dudgeon.

Things got worse. Professor Branestawm's ingenious ideas were working splendidly. But the Pagwellians were even more ingenious in using them in all sorts of unexpected ways. People had themselves a ball. They got up to larks. They enjoyed themselves far too much. And poor old Pagwell Council was in a terrible state.

'Inflation will overtake us again!' moaned the Mayor.

'We shall have to charge rates again!' cried the Town Clerk.

It was no use calling Colonel Dedshott and the Catapult Cavaliers this time. Attacking the dodgem cars or setting about roundabouts or charging the traffic wardens wouldn't help at all.

Professor Branestawm waved his hands and his spectacles flew about.

'Can't you invent a machine for putting things back as they were?' groaned the Mayor.

Professor Branestawm couldn't. But what he could do was invent a rival Fun Fair with much more exciting things in it, to lure away the Pagwellians from the road-sweeping dodgem cars, the hole-mending, the traffic warden game and the water-pumping roundabouts.

And that is what he did.

But it took Great Pagwell simply ages to get back to having the roads swept and mended by road-sweeping and mending men, and having proper traffic wardens putting tickets on cars, and letting the pumping station do without its roundabouts. And some of the people who used to do those jobs didn't want to come back so that the Catapult Cavaliers had to be pressed into service temporarily, and students had to do the jobs in their holidays. But at last Great Pagwell was itself again, with nice expensive rates and inflation doing its thing once more.

And Professor Branestawm had the great satisfaction of knowing that for once it wasn't his inventions that went wrong but the people who used them. It was a lovely change.

From *Professor Branestawm Round the Bend*

Professor Branestawm
and the Secret Agents

Professor Branestawm took to the stage for the first time during Christmas 1979 with Nottingham Playhouse's musical adaptation of some of his *Incredible Adventures*. In this short extract from the script, the Professor's interest in unusual foreign accents nearly leads him into deep trouble, when he and Colonel Dedshott are held up by two enemy agents from Crashbania, who are trying to steal the Professor's plans for a new secret weapon ...

(*Professor Branestawm and Colonel Dedshott are engrossed in discussing how the Professor can invent a Loch-Ness-type monster that will attract tourists to Pagwell, when Raincoat and Beard and Ears, two thugs disguised as secret agents from Crashbania, enter, carrying guns. They are obviously heavily disguised in false beards, etc., and speak with thick foreign accents.*)

BEARD AND EARS Okay, you guys, up against the wall.

RAINCOAT Not a word, or it'll be curtains for you.

(*The Professor, oblivious of danger, looks at the two men with interest, but Colonel Dedshott immediately puts both hands up and starts to move gingerly off stage.*)

DEDSHOTT Don't shoot. I'm going.

RAINCOAT Stay where you are!

PROFESSOR Did you say it'll be curtains for us?

RAINCOAT That's right.

PROFESSOR That'll be nice . . . Mrs, um, er Flittersnoop was only saying the other day that we need some new, um, ah, curtains . . .

BEARD AND EARS Shut up, wise guy. He don't mean curtains. He means *coytains*.

PROFESSOR (*imitating his accent*) *Coytains*, eh?

RAINCOAT You betcha.

PROFESSOR Most, um, ah, interesting.

RAINCOAT What is?

PROFESSOR The way he says 'curtains'.

BEARD AND EARS (*with a threatening gesture*) I'll give you interesting . . .

PROFESSOR I thought you were going to give me curtains, but would you, um, er, allow me to look in your mouth while you, um, ah, say that?

BEARD AND EARS Like fun I will.

PROFESSOR That really is most, um, er, kind. (*He takes hold of Beard and Ears's lower jaw and looks into his mouth.*)

Now just say 'curtains' again for me, will you?

BEARD AND EARS Get your hands offa me, burster!

PROFESSOR Oh, that's just as good – '*burster*'. Again please.

RAINCOAT Look, what's with you, mister?

PROFESSOR It's just that I'm um, er, interested in languages, you know, foreign accents and all that. I've never heard anyone say, er, um, 'curtains' and 'buster' like that before, though now I come to, um, ah, think about it, it is similar to how they say it in Outer Crashbania, and I want to, um, ah, see just where his tongue is when he makes that 'ur' sound.

RAINCOAT (*evidently growing impatient*) Do the 'curtains' for him, Beard and Ears.

BEARD AND EARS I don't want this nutcase in my mouth. Do it yourself.

PROFESSOR Oh, no. It's you I want to look at. He doesn't do it half so well.

BEARD AND EARS Oh . . . all right. *Coytains.*

(*The Professor peers into his mouth. Dedshott, fascinated, steps forward to look too.*)

PROFESSOR Again, please.

BEARD AND EARS *Coytains.*

PROFESSOR Buster.

BEARD AND EARS *Burster.*

(*Beard and Ear's false beard accidentally comes off as the Professor peers into his mouth.*)

PROFESSOR Um, ah, your beard appears to have, um, ah, er, moulted. How very interesting.

(*Beard and Ears hurriedly puts it back on.*)

RAINCOAT That's enough of all this. We've got work to do too, you know.

PROFESSOR Really, and what sort of, er, work do you do, Mr, er . . .?

RAINCOAT We stick people up.

PROFESSOR Stick them up where?

RAINCOAT Stick them up with guns.

PROFESSOR Really? I'd use glue.

BEARD AND EARS No, not stick them up – you know, STICK EM UP!

(*He points his gun threateningly at them. Colonel Dedshott shoots up his hands again and backs off.*)

PROFESSOR (*looking puzzled*) Like . . . not curtains, but *coytains*. Dear me, this really is a most, um, er, confusing morning. But carry on Mr, um, er . . ., and, er, stick someone up.

BEARD AND EARS We are.

PROFESSOR Are what?

RAINCOAT Sticking someone up.

PROFESSOR Who?

BEARD AND EARS AND RAINCOAT *You!*

PROFESSOR Oh?

BEARD AND EARS Yeah. We're sticking you up and we're telling you to hand over the plans for the new . . . What's the thing called?

RAINCOAT Tink.

BEARD AND EARS I *am* tinking.

PROFESSOR Tank.

BEARD AND EARS Yeah, that's it. Tank. Hand over the plans.

PROFESSOR Plans?

RAINCOAT Yeah

PROFESSOR There aren't any, er, um, ah, plans. I just made the tank up as I went along.

BEARD AND EARS *No plans?*

PROFESSOR No.

BEARD AND EARS There gotta be!

PROFESSOR Sorry.

BEARD AND EARS Curses! What do we do now?

RAINCOAT Well ... if there's no plans ... we'll have to take you with us.

PROFESSOR Me?

RAINCOAT That's right.

PROFESSOR Where to?

RAINCOAT Crashbania.

PROFESSOR Most terribly, er, kind, but I've had my holiday for this year.

BEARD AND EARS This won't be no holiday, burster!

PROFESSOR *Very* nice! You said it again.

(*He steps towards Beard and Ears to have another look in his mouth.*)

DEDSHOTT Don't you see, Branestawm! They want you to go to Crashbania to make tanks for them and not for our Army!

PROFESSOR You mean they want to, er um, ah, *kidnap* me?

DEDSHOTT That's right.

PROFESSOR But that's um, ah, pre-, um ah, posterous!

(*He turns to Raincoat and Beard and Ears*) Why didn't you say so before?

The Unexpected Tale of
Professor Flittersnoop

Professor Branestawm was walking down Pagwell High Street. And he looked extremely odd. He had buttons on his coat instead of the usual safety pins. His trousers were smartly creased right down the centre instead of sideways all over the place. His tie was neatly tied and he had his hat on the right way round. He looked nearly as elegant as a whole packet of new pins done up in a gift wrap.

Nobody would have recognized him. Nobody, that is, except his old friend, Colonel Dedshott of the Catapult Cavaliers, who was used to spotting not-done-up buttons on soldiers on parade and things like that. He penetrated the Professor's disguise in a moment.

'Branestawm, my word, hullo, what!' he cried. He got off his horse, which he was riding for a treat. 'Going to a party or something?'

'Oh, ah, hullo, Dedshott,' said the Professor. 'You are surprised at my, er, um, somewhat strange appearance no doubt. It's a new invention of mine. You must come round tomorrow and I'll explain. I can't stop now, I'm on my way to lecture at the Pagwell Science Institute.'

He shot off down the road in the direction of the Library, in mistake for the Science Institute. But as it was really at the Library he was supposed to lecture, things were better than they seemed.

'Ha, hrrmph!' said Colonel Dedshott, wondering what sort of an invention could make the Professor look so un-professorish. He cantered off home, to wait until tomorrow when he would hear all about it from the Professor and probably not understand any of it.

Ding dong ding dong, clang bing a ding dong! the Professor's specially invented alarm clock went off. It sounded rather more like Robin Hood's wedding in technicolour than an alarm clock. But it woke the Professor most definitely up, which ordinary alarm clocks sometimes found it a bit of a job to do.

'A-a-a-a-h,' yawned the Professor. 'Oh bother, time to get up. This getting dressed business is such a waste of time. Doing it every morning and then un-doing it again at night. Why doesn't somebody invent . . .'

He got the answer to that question with a noise like ten squeaky sewing-machines trying to beat eggs, followed by assorted pops and mixed bangs as the getting-you-dressed machine he had invented and forgotten about put him rapidly into his clothes, which it had pressed during the night. It brushed him down, brushed him up, washed his face, combed his hair, cleaned his teeth with a special rotary tooth-brush and pineapple-flavoured toothpaste, polished his shoes and then left off with a satisfied sigh as if someone had carefully let the air out of a balloon.

'Ha, yes, of course. I invented that,' said the Professor. 'Clever of me, and it works splendidly.' He went downstairs, forgot about his breakfast and became all soaked up in a new invention for straightening curly bananas.

Mrs Flittersnoop, who had been staying with her sister Aggie for a few days, finished the last bit of washing-up the Professor had left. It wasn't much really because he used only one plate, one cup and a spoon for everything, though she was a bit cross because he had put the little weeny teapot for one in the cupboard where the large visitors' teapot should have been. Then, pushing a nice cup of tea and a round of toast through the inventory window, where it got mixed up with sliced straightened bananas, she went up to make the Professor's bed.

'There now!' she exclaimed when she saw the getting-you-dressed machine. 'If it isn't another of the Professor's inventions he's been at while I've been away. I wonder if it's a machine for making the bed.' She pushed a little lever very gingerly, thinking there would be no harm in getting the bed made without having to do it.

Of course, she ought to have known better, did Mrs Flittersnoop. Her having housekeepered for the

Professor ever since goodness knows when. And in two seconds she did know better this time. But two seconds is about half an hour too long to take to know better where the Professor's inventions are concerned, they being a bit on the hasty side.

Squeaketty squeaketty popetty pop, boing, bzzoing wallopetty smack, puff puff! Mrs Flittersnoop found herself in bed, while her best blue and white spotted dress and all her other clothes were industriously pressed and put away in the machine. The Professor had arranged it so that the machine not only got you dressed in the morning but put you to bed very considerately at night.

'Goodness gracious!' Mrs Flittersnoop tried to exclaim. But the machine popped a large sweet into her mouth, rapidly read half a page of a very scientific story at her and put out the light, which made no difference as it was daylight.

'Oh, glumph, ym, ym, glop!' gasped Mrs Flittersnoop. She sprang out of the bed, swallowed the sweet, dashed into her room and hurriedly put on more clothes including her second-best blue and white spotted dress, which was exactly the same as the one the machine had got inside it, but not quite so smart.

Only just in time. *Rat tat*, Colonel Dedshott was knocking at the door, ready to have the new invention explained to him. When Mrs Flittersnoop opened the door he thought she didn't look quite so neat and tidy as usual. This was partly due to her not having entirely recovered from the attentions of the getting-you-dressed machine and partly due to the blue and white spotted dress being her second-best. For a moment the Colonel thought the Professor's invention for making him look smart had something, but goodness knows what, to do with making Mrs Flittersnoop look not quite so smart. But by then the Professor was five-eighths of the way through explaining his banana-straightening machine and Colonel Dedshott hardly had time to get his thoughts sorted out before his head began to go round and round, only this time rather faster than usual.

'Of course, the bananas have to be peeled first,' said the Professor, 'otherwise the resistance co-efficient of the peel operates counterwise to the strightening effect of the, er, straightener.'

'Marvellous!' gasped the Colonel, wondering how on earth bananas could turn the Professor out looking like a tailor's dummy got up for a heavy party.

The Professor, of course, had forgotten about the getting-you-dressed machine again. He had found that thinking about two inventions at once was apt to cause unheard of things to happen, though of course they were all too probably likely to happen even if he thought of no inventions at all, which he was too clever to do.

'Hrrmph!' said the Colonel on the way home. 'Now I suppose he'll write a book about the influence of fruit on people's dress or something. I don't know how he does it, my word I don't.'

That evening the Professor, still thinking about banana-straightening, forgot about the getting-you-dressed-and-putting-you-to-bed machine. So he undressed himself in the ordinary way by hand, and got into bed leaving his clothes absolutely everywhere.

Next morning *Ding dong, etc*, went the wake-up chimes and oh good gracious! *Poppety flump, whiz*, the Professor was rapidly dressed in Mrs Flittersnoop's best blue and white spotted dress, with trimmings, because those were the clothes the machine had all pressed and ready from the day before.

The Professor didn't notice anything. There are some things even a professor can't do, and thinking about best blue and white spotted dresses that don't belong to them and straight and curly bananas, all at the same time, is absolutely one of them, as any professor will tell you if you ask him. Anyway he was in too much of a hurry to go out and buy some very long skinny screws for his banana machine even to wait for breakfast. He picked up a sausage off the table and was off to the ironmonger's before Mrs Flittersnoop could stop him.

'Oh deary, deary good gracious me!' she cried, wishing she had stayed at her sister Aggie's. 'There he goes, all got up in my best blue and white.' She guessed that had something to do with the getting-you-dressed machine because she had become slightly quick at guessing things about the Professor's inventions, so as to be prepared when something drastic was likely to happen, which it nearly always was. 'I must do something to stop him indeed I must, or goodness knows what people will think,'

She hurriedly rang up Colonel Dedshott, who immediately organized a handful of Catapult Cavaliers to spread out through the streets of Pagwell, head the Professor off and bring him safely home. 'You'll know him by the blue and white spotted dress and five pairs of spectacles,' barked the Colonel.

'Try the ironmonger's first!' shouted Mrs Flittersnoop down the telephone, not knowing the Colonel had already rung off and was getting his horse out to join in the hunt. Then, reckoning that the housekeeping must go on, never mind what, she set off in her second-best blue and white spotted dress for the Pagwell Supermarket.

The Catapult Cavaliers were, of course, very good at fanning out through places because of their military training. But they had rather mixed ideas of where Professor Branestawm might have got to. Some fanned out round Pagwell Park where a cricket match was occurring which they felt the Professor might just possibly be looking at and which they rather wanted to look at themselves. Others fanned themselves into a cinema where there was a morning performance, feeling that even if the Professor wasn't there, the time wouldn't be wasted as they wanted to see the film themselves. They were very resourceful, were the Catapult Cavaliers. Still others thought the Professor might be resting in Pagwell Gardens or watching the barges whiz by on Pagwell Canal, and they fanned themselves all round those places. And a few of them, having no idea at all where the Professor was to be found, fanned themselves out through the streets of Great Pagwell, diligently inspecting the scenery for signs of the Professor, particularly those parts of the scenery which were young and pretty and wearing mini skirts, just in case they were blue and white spotted ones.

On the way to the ironmonger's Professor Branestawm met Dr Mumpzanmeazle. He was on his way back from a little girl whose mum thought she had exaggerated measles, but which turned out to be spots of her lipstick the little girl had been trying to make herself look special with.

The Doctor saw at once that something was wrong with the Professor, without listening to his chest or giving him a thermometer to suck or making him say 'ah' or anything. He was mighty good at spots, was the Doctor, even blue and white ones.

'Whatever are you wearing that for?' he said, guessing the Professor didn't know. 'Come to my surgery and have a cup of coffee.'

'Dear me!' said the Professor, over his third cup of coffee and tenth custard tart. He was hungry from having had no breakfast, except the sausage, which he had tried to put in his pocket anyway. But Mrs Flittersnoop's best blue and white spotted dress didn't have pockets so the sausage had fallen by the wayside so to speak and was appreciatively munched up by a spare dog. 'Dear me!' he said. 'I didn't know I had a suit like this,' which of course he hadn't.

Then he explained his getting-you-dressed-and-putting-you-to-bed machine to Dr Mumpzanmeazle though even he couldn't explain how it got hold of Mrs Flittersnoop's dress.

'This is how it operates,' explained the Professor, finishing the Doctor's custard tart by mistake and drawing complicated diagrams on an already fearfully complicated chart of a red, white and blue man which showed you how people's muscles worked.

'Here is the trouser remover, presser and replacer,' said the Professor, drawing concentric circles round the chart's legs. 'This is where the jacket is hung up, any missing buttons re-, um, placed,' two triangles and an oval on the chart's shoulders. 'A reversing lever here,' two dots on the chart's nose, 'enables the machine to undress one at night instead of dressing one in the morning. There is also, er, provision for turning socks right way out, arranging a shirt the right way up, a necktie un-tier and re-tier, a bootlace disentangler and a woolly vest putter-oner.'

Dr Mumpzanmeazle listened carefully and his head didn't go round at all, not even half way. He had got used to hearing complicated scientific explanations when he was studying to be a doctor. He could understand the thickest descriptions and soon make short work of long words.

'Excellent, my dear Professor,' he said and at the bottom of the chart, which now had levers and springs and trapdoors instead of muscles, he wrote, 'To be taken twice daily, morning and evening' in the proper doctors' writing which nobody but chemists can read.

He thought the machine was a very good idea. He was always having to get up at ridiculous times of the night to go dashing off to people who were either frightfully ill without notice or thought they were, or to inconsiderate ladies who would go having babies before breakfast.

'Can't you make me one of these things?' he said. 'Be a great help in my practice.'

So the Professor said, 'Yes, yes, of course,' and off he went, wearing the Doctor's second-best raincoat to hide Mrs Flittersnoop's best blue and white spotted dress, which it didn't do entirely, the Doctor being rather given to shorty raincoats while Mrs Flittersnoop definitely favoured longy dresses.

Mrs Flittersnoop was in Pagwell Supermarket, trying to make up her mind whether it was cheaper to get a family sized packet of soapflakes with sixpence off and a free bar of chocolate; or a giant sized packet with nothing off, but coupons for saving up to get fish knives at half price; or four large sized packets at rather more than three quarters price tied together with three tubes of toothpaste for the price of two.

Suddenly she was surrounded by three Catapult Cavaliers, two of whom took an arm each and escorted her with forcible politeness out of the supermarket while the third marched behind in case she got away.

Of course they thought she was Professor Branestawm. You could hardly blame them. There was the spotted blue and white dress the Colonel had told them to look for. And there were at least two pairs of spectacles. One was the pair Mrs Flittersnoop always wore for looking at sensational bargain prices in supermarkets and the other was a pair of sunglasses she was going to buy for sister Aggie who was on the brink of going off for a seaside holiday and expected rather a lot of sunshine.

'How dare you!' cried Mrs Flittersnoop, stamping on the Cavaliers' feet with her heels, which they didn't feel anything to speak of because her heels weren't very sharp and the boots were considerably thick, 'Let me go this minute.'

'All right, Professor Branestawm, no need to take on so,' said the right hand Cavalier.

'You're in good 'ands sir,' said the left hand one.

'You come with us and we'll see you're all right, Prof,' added the marching-behind one.

'I am not Professor Branestawm,' protested Mrs

Flittersnoop, putting on the sunglasses on top of her own spectacles and so making herself look rather much like him.

'That's all right, sir,' said the right hand Cavalier, winking at the others. 'But you come with us just the same and get your own clothes on instead of that dress, which don't really suit you like, if you understand me, Professor.'

Mrs Flittersnoop immediately stopped seeing red and began to see daylight, of which there was certainly a great deal about, as they now out of the supermarket and in Pagwell Square.

'Listen to me, young man,' she said, going all practical and determined. 'I'm Mrs Flittersnoop, Professor Branestawm's housekeeper. He went out this morning wearing one of my dresses by mistake. It was to do with one of those inventions of his. If you're looking for him you'd best start at the ironmonger's.'

At this the three Cavaliers looked at each other and they began to see large quantities of daylight too. There was a bit of army sort of talk between them and plenty of explaining talk from Mrs Flittersnoop.

Then they all began to laugh.

'Dear oh dearie me!' said Mrs Flittersnoop. 'It's the first time three young men have wanted to take me out at once, yes, indeed, I'm sure.'

And as they were just outside the Geat pagwell Ye Olde Bunne Shoppe, they decided to go in and have ye olde coffee and bunnes together.

'But what about the Prof?' said one of the Cavaliers.

'Oh, he'll be all right,' said Mrs Flittersnoop. 'The ironmonger, where he went to buy screws, will have seen what's wrong and he'll be home by now. And if he's damaged my best blue and white spotted dress this being my second-best if you see what I mean – I can always get another at Ginnibag & Knitwoddle's sale.'

Of course the Professor had got home safely, though it was with the aid of Dr Mumpzanmeazle's raincoat and not with the ironmonger's help. And when Mrs Flittersnoop arrived back he was straightening bananas quite happily in his inventory, still in her best blue and white spotted, which was still as good as new, and quite undamaged, unlikely as it seemed.

So all was well that ended not too badly. But Dr Mumpzanmeazle had an absolute time of it with the Professor's getting-you-dressed-and-putting-you-to-bed machine, which would keep getting him up at three in the morning and then putting him straight back to bed again whether any patients wanted their temperatures taken or not.

From *The Peculiar Triumph of Professor Branestawm*

Professor Flittersnoop and Mrs Branestawm

In the last story Professor Branestawm changed clothes with Mrs Flittersnoop, by mistake. That was all the fault of his getting-you-dressed machine, of course, but now here's a trick you can do yourselves, by which the Professor and Mrs Flittersnoop change clothes by magic.

This piece of magic is a simplified, and adapted version of an illusion devised a long time ago by a celebrated American magician, U.F. Grant.

The magician has on the stage with him a boy and a girl. He gives the boy some clothes to dress up as Professor Branestawm. Then he gives the girl clothes to dress up as Mrs Flittersnoop.

The boy and girl stand one on each side of the stage.

'Now,' says the magician, 'I want you to change places.' And the Professor and Mrs Flittersnoop each walk across the stage to opposite sides.

'Oh, that's a dull way of changing places,' says the magician. 'Do it by magic.' He claps his hands. Professor Branestawm takes off his disguise and the audience see that he is really the girl. Mrs Flittersnoop does the same and turns out to be the boy.

HOW TO DO IT

You will need, of course, a boy and a girl. They should be the same size and height. You will also need a second boy. He must be the same size and height as the other two and he should wear the same kind of trousers and shoes as the other boy. He should also, if possible, have the same colour and style of hair. Your audience do not know of the existence of this second boy and he is behind a screen or off stage at the start of the trick.

You bring on the other boy and the girl and you say you are going to get them to dress up as Professor Branestawm and Mrs Flittersnoop. You give the boy clothes for the Professor. These consist of a long, loose-fitting grey coat. The kind of overall coat that painters and warehousemen wear is ideal and can be bought at shops that sell overalls and boiler suits. The coat should be long enough to reach right to the ground and be rather too big for the boy. Then you will need a comic mask, which you can buy at a novelty shop. This mask should have a pair of spectacles on it. If it hasn't you can make a pair from cardboard and stick them on. You will also need a large felt hat that will come down well over the boy's ears and hide his hair.

The boy takes these things and goes behind the screen. But he doesn't put them on. Instead the second boy puts them on and comes out on to the stage.

To cover the time the boy will take to put the clothes on you explain that the Professor takes a little time to dress and that you mustn't hurry him or otherwise he may put his clothes on upside-down or inside-out.

When the second boy, dressed as the Professor, comes out, he stands on the side of the stage. You then give to the girl some clothes for her to dress up as Mrs Flittersnoop. These consist of a long, loose overall, buttoning down the front. It should reach right to the ground and be a bit too large for the girl, just as the Professor's coat was too large for the boy. The overall for Mrs Flittersnoop should be a bright colour and, if possible, of flowered material. You also give her a suitable mask and a large floppy hat that will hide her hair. The girl, by the way, has to have short hair.

The girl takes the clothes and goes behind the screen. But she doesn't put the Mrs Flittersnoop clothes on. Instead the boy, the one the audience saw to start with and who is waiting there, puts on the Mrs Flittersnoop clothes. He comes out and stands on the other side of the stage.

And just as you made up the time to allow the Professor to dress, you explain to the audience that ladies always take a bit of time to dress, and you can't hurry ladies or otherwise they forget to draw their eyebrows straight or leave something behind.

You now have the boy the audience have seen, dressed as Mrs Flittersnoop, and you have the second boy (whom the audience haven't seen) dressed as the Professor. Behind the screen the girl has put on a duplicate coat and mask of the Professor. She also has in her hand four pairs of spectacles, dummy ones, of course, or toy ones. She waits there unseen.

You now look at the boy dressed as Professor Branestawm and say, 'My dear Professor, you're so absent-minded. But then we all know you are, and you've forgotten some of your spectacles. You've got only one pair and you should have five. Please go and get the other pairs as we want you all complete.'

The boy dressed as the Professor unbuttons the lower part of his coat and feels in his trousers' pocket, then waves his hand and says, 'Oh dear, yes, tut, tut. How careless of me! Excuse me while I get the other pairs.' He goes behind the screen. The girl, dressed as the Professor, puts on the boy's Professor hat and comes on waving the four pairs of spectacles.

You now have the two children the audience saw

to begin with, dressed as Mrs Flittersnoop and the Professor. But of course it is the girl who is dressed as the Professor and the boy who is dressed as Mrs Flittersnoop.

You then ask the children to change places and they cross over to opposite sides of the stage. When you say, 'Let's do it by magic,' you clap your hands and the children take off the disguises showing that Mrs Flittersnoop is the boy and the Professor is the girl.

The important thing here is that right up to the last minute, the audience are allowed to see that the person in the Professor Branestawm disguise is a boy and they naturally assume it is the boy they first saw, as they don't know what is going to happen. It seems quite a natural bit of fun to make the Professor forget his spectacles and as he simply goes behind the screen and immediately comes back the audience have no idea that it is really the girl disguised as the Professor who comes out with the spectacles.

To make everything quite clear let me sum up what happens.

1. Boy and girl on stage in front of audience.
2. Second boy behind screen. Also behind screen second Professor coat, mask, and four pairs of spectacles.
3. Boy on stage goes behind screen with Professor disguise but other boy puts it on and comes out.
4. Girl on stage goes behind screen with Mrs Flittersnoop disguise but boy who is there puts

it on and comes on stage.

5. Girl behind screen puts on second Professor coat and mask and picks up the four pairs of spectacles.

6. Boy on stage dressed as Professor goes behind screen to fetch spectacles. But girl takes off his hat, puts it on and goes on stage carrying the four pairs of spectacles.

7. Boy on stage is now dressed as Mrs Flittersnoop and girl on stage is dressed as the Professor.

8. They cross over and change places.

9. They remove their disguises and show that the one dressed as Mrs Flittersnoop is now the boy and the one dressed as the Professor is the girl.

You may find it helpful to have someone behind the screen to help your actors put the clothes on. But they obviously have to have time to dress, and you, the magician, explain that to the audience.

Rehearse this piece of magic carefully so that it can be done calmly without hurry and you'll find it will produce gasps of astonishment from the audience as the Professor and Mrs Flittersnoop apparently magically change places.

From *Vanishing Ladies and Other Magic*

The Big Zipper

I, um, ah, believe it is your birthday today, Mrs Flittersnoop,' said the Professor one breakfast-time.

'Yes, indeed, I'm sure, sir,' smiled Mrs Flittersnoop, who had entered a little note in the Professor's diary to remind him of that interesting fact. Of course, the Professor would probably have forgotten to look in his diary, only Mrs Flittersnoop had put it under his plate to make sure.

'I, um, ah, think this calls for a little, um, celebration,' said the Professor. 'Would you care to meet me for tea this afternoon at Ginnibag & Knitwoddle's restaurant?'

Mrs Flittersnoop said she'd be delighted.

'I've got a little shopping to do, sir, if that's all right with you, so I'll meet you in the restaurant. Shall we say half past four?'

So the Professor said 'half past four'. Mrs

Flittersnoop cleared away the breakfast things and went into the kitchen, while the Professor went into his inventory.

Strangely enough, Professor Branestawm remembered about taking Mrs Flittersnoop to tea.

'Ginnibag & Knitwoddle's at half past four,' he said and off he went. When he got to Ginnibag & Knitwoddle there was a notice on the double doors at the front saying 'Please use other door.' It meant, of course, that you were to use the right-hand door and not the left-hand one, because that one was being mended and wouldn't open.

But Professor Branestawm, always ready to obey polite requests, thought it meant 'Don't use this entrance,' and he went round the back of the building to the other entrance to the store.

But the double doors at that entrance also had one door out of action and a notice saying 'Please use other door.'

'Dear me,' said the Professor. 'It seems one cannot get into the store although it's open; though I fail to see how a store can be open, if you cannot use the doors to get in.'

Just then a lady with a shopping trolley and two little girls swept in through the openable door and politely held it open for the Professor, so he got in after all.

The Professor arrived at the lift, only to be met by another notice. (Ginnibag & Knitwoddle were pretty smart at notices.) It said 'We regret lift out of order.'

'Oh well, I suppose I must walk up,' said the Professor.

He went over to the stairs, but found they were cluttered up with no end of ladders, buckets and men in overalls, and another notice saying 'Stairs closed. Please use the lift.'

'But the lift is regrettably out of order,' said the Professor.

'Ah, no sir,' said a gentleman in a pale suit and a wide smile, who seemed to be in charge of all these notices. 'That is to say we have another lift, straight through the ironmongery department.'

'Oh, um, ah, thank you,' said the Professor, but he failed to go straight through the ironmongery department because he remembered he wanted some special screws, which, as it turned out, Ginnibag & Knitwoddle were disinclined to stock.

At last the Professor got into the lift, but got out at the first floor instead of waiting for the fourth and found himself in the dress department, which was packed with so many rows of ladies dresses, that the customers could hardly get in. And there, behind one of the rows, was Mrs Flittersnoop.

'I, um, ah, thought we were to meet in the restaurant,' said the Professor. 'I don't think they serve tea here.'

Mrs Flittersnoop was just going to answer when an extremely haughty lady with a very high hair-do swept up and asked, 'Can I help you?' in a very well-off voice.

'Well,' said Mrs Flittersnoop, 'I was looking for a dress.'

This didn't seem to surprise tall hair-do very much as the place was stuffed tight with dresses and suits and caftans and things called separates, which you could wear one at a time or both together, according to what sort of weather it was going to be or whom you were going to meet.

'Something not too expensive,' added Mrs Flitter-snoop cautiously, having been slightly frightened by a price ticket she'd looked at.

'Oh, yes,' said tall hair-do in a voice that suggested Mrs Flittersnoop was a refugee from a local dustbin. She beckoned with a long skinny finger and another lady with a rather lower hair-do came up.

Professor Branestawm watched all this with professorial interest. He thought if the height of the sales ladies' hair-do's was adjusted according to the price of the dresses they sold, possibly in a sale, when things went very cheap, you might get served by a bald-headed lady, but he didn't think that would be very suitable somehow.

Meantime Mrs Flittersnoop and medium hair-do had collected a selection of dresses, and vanished with them into a little room marked 'Ladies changing room'.

Professor Branestawm was just wondering what they changed ladies into in that room and thinking he didn't want Mrs Flittersnoop changed because she suited him very well as she was, when Mrs Flitter-snoop came out *very* much changed indeed. She was wearing a smart dress with a fetching pattern of coloured chains all over it.

'How do you like it, Professor?' she asked.

'Oh, um, ah, er, nice,' said the Professor, who liked the chains, but would have preferred cog-wheels.

Just then a lady in a skinny little white hat emerged from the woodwork and hissed to Mrs Flittersnoop, 'Don't buy it!'

Professor Branestawm wondered if she was someone employed by Ginnibag & Knitwoddle to discourage customers from buying anything that was too cheap, so that they'd buy something more expensive. But it turned out that the lady was actually a friend of Mrs Flittersnoop's.

'Don't buy it!' she repeated. 'It's got a back zip.'

Professor Branestawm wondered what particularly vicious kind of thing a back zip could be that made it so undesirable for Mrs Flittersnoop to buy a dress that had one.

'So difficult to do up by oneself,' said the lady.

'Oh, why, yes, indeed, I'm sure,' said Mrs Flittersnoop. 'You're quite right. Never depend on others if you can help it, I always say.'

Mrs Flittersnoop couldn't bear the idea of asking Professor Branestawm to zip up her dress, so she always bought ones that did up down the front or could be put on without undoing or doing up.

Professor Branestawm stood there with his head beginning to go round and round very slowly. All this talk of back zips and separates and other ladies' dressology had so confused him that he didn't realize that an idea for a new invention had let itself into his head while he wasn't looking. It wasn't until he and Mrs Flittersnoop were seated in Ginnibag & Knitwoddle's restaurant that he realized what had happened.

'Pot of tea for two and some pastries,' said Mrs Flittersnoop to the waitress.

'I'll, um, ah, have some tomato soup,' said the Professor, forgetting it wasn't lunch-time, as he had just realized he had an invention idea rattling round inside his head.

'Zipping dresses up the back is apt to be inconvenient if you are alone. Is that not so, Mrs Flittersnoop?'

'Yes, indeed, I'm sure, sir,' said Mrs Flittersnoop. 'That's why I've bought another dress that does up down the front.'

Just then the waitress put a bowl of tomato soup in front of the Professor, who stirred it with one of his five pairs of spectacles, put the others on, looked at the soup and said to the waitress.

'Take it away! Whoever heard of having soup at tea-time?'

Now it should have been the waitress's turn to have her head go round and round, but it didn't because she was used to dealing with rummy customers. She just took the soup away, brought the tea and pastries and Mrs Flittersnoop set about being mother, which ladies can do without having any children as long as they have a pot of tea. Then the Professor set about telling her about the idea that had come to him in the dress department for a special zip-you-up machine.

'Well, sir,' said Mrs Flittersnoop, having another jam tart, 'if I might make so bold, sir, there is already something to help you zip up a dress. It is a piece of cord with a little hook on the end. You just hook it through the tag on the zip and pull the cord over your shoulder.'

'Tut, tut,' said the Professor, putting a piece of scone into his tea in mistake for sugar. 'I don't think ladies should have to, er, mess about with bits of string in order to zip themselves up. It is not at all ladylike.'

'Well, sir,' said Mrs Flittersnoop, 'I must say I've never used one myself seeing as how I always have dresses that do up down the front.'

'With my idea,' went on the Professor, 'you have an arrangement fixed to the wall. You simply stand with your back against it, press a button and up goes your zip. Then', he took a drink of tea and two of his pairs of glasses fell into the cup, 'to unzip yourself you do exactly the same only this time the machine zips the zip down instead of up. You must, of course,' he wagged a finger and the waitress thought he wanted another scone to drop into his tea, 'you must press the button to make sure the zipping attachment is at the bottom if you wish to be zipped up, or at the top if you wish to be unzipped down, you understand?'

'Yes, indeed, I'm sure, sir,' said Mrs Flittersnoop, who didn't understand anything except that, thank goodness, she wouldn't have to use the Professor's machine as she always had button-down-the-front dresses.

Professor Branestawm was demonstrating his dress zipping and unzipping machine to the Great Pagwell Ladies' Social Club. The device was fastened to the wall where it looked something like a 'try your strength' machine that you have to hit with a hammer, something like a rather bad-tempered weighing machine, and something like the thing that tells you what the weather isn't going to be like tomorrow.

'Would some lady be kind enough to step forward so that I can demonstrate the device?' asked the Professor, looking over and under and through various pairs of spectacles.

The ladies all looked at one another and felt rather as if a conjurer was asking them to help with a trick. Nobody moved because they were all waiting for someone else to get up. Then, as nobody got up, all the ladies stood up at once, except one who was wearing a T-shirt and trousers and who couldn't therefore be zipped or unzipped up the back. They all said 'Ah!', and then sat down again.

'I, um, ah, think perhaps I might make a choice,' said the Professor, who could see the demonstration never getting off the ground, so to speak. He pointed to a young lady in a pink dress, who giggled, got up and went over to the machine. She stood with her back to it and the Professor pressed a button. There was a click.

'The zip-upping attachment has now attached itself to the tag of this lady's zip,' he explained. 'As her dress is already zipped up the machine will now unzip it.' He pressed another button, there was a whizzing sound and the young lady's nice pink dress came unzipped and fell off.

For a moment there was a moderate consternation. But as the young lady had no end of underclothes on, and as there weren't any gentlemen present, except Professor Branestawm, whose five pairs of spectacles had all fallen down over his eyes so he couldn't see anything but fog, the situation wasn't that drastic. Two other ladies helped the young lady in the pink dress, who had gone rather pink herself, back into her dress and the machine promptly zipped it up again, to a slight round of applause, though whether this was for the machine, for the Professor, or for the young lady, isn't certain.

'I, um, er, think that seems satisfactory,' said the Professor.

Then there was a rush of ladies of all kinds to try the machine. Dresses were zipped up and down with the speed of excitable lightning. And, of course, all the ladies wanted one of the Professor's remarkable self-zipping machines for themselves

'A most satisfactory and practical invention I, um, ah, think,' said the Professor to Mrs Flittersnoop later. 'I have made my special zipping machines for the Mayoress, for Lady Pagwell, for Miss Frenzie, the Vicar's wife and many other ladies.' Maisie and Daisie, the Vicar's twin daughters, said they didn't want two machines, or even one, because they could always zip each other up and down, and often wore things that didn't zip anyway.

'Yes, indeed, I'm sure, sir,' said Mrs Flittersnoop, half-wishing she had dresses that zipped up the back, so that she could have had one of the Professor's wonderful machines. But she didn't half-wish for long. Suddenly there came a ring at the door, another one on the phone and people banging on the window.

'Come quickly, Professor!' 'Help, Professor!' 'Urgent, hurry Professor!' came the demands. Panic seemed to be taking place everywhere.

At the vicarage yelps were coming from the best bedroom. The Vicar's wife was up against the ceiling, where the zipping-up machine had zipped her and wouldn't let go.

At her home Miss Frenzie was on the floor apparently looking for lost property, but in fact it was because the zipper had zipped her and her dress down on to the carpet.

At the mayoral residence the Mayoress was half-way up the wall and the Mayor was all the way up it in despair.

All over Pagwell, schoolteachers, librarians, non-librarians, housewives and other assorted ladies were trapped in unladylike positions by the Professor's machines.

The Professor clapped on his hat, missed and clapped it on Mrs Flittersnoop.

'Ring up Colonel Dedshott!' gasped the Professor. 'Tell him to go and help the Mayor's wife!' He shot out and Mrs Flittersnoop got to the telephone just in time to answer a call from a lady who thought she was ringing the dairy. To save time, Mrs Flittersnoop took an order for two pints of milk, half a pint of cream, two dozen brown eggs and a white sliced loaf, then said, 'Wrong number, I'm afraid,' rang off, and got on to the Colonel.

Professor Branestawm dashed in to see

Commander Hardaport (Retired), and sent him off to help Miss Frenzie, while he tore off to the rescue of the Vicar's wife. Mrs Flittersnoop rang the Fire Brigade and the police, and soon that half of Pagwell that wasn't on the floor or up on the ceiling in the clutches of the Professor's Zippers, was on its way to rescue those who were.

Colonel Dedshott burst into the Mayor's house waving his sword. He dashed up to the Zipper and took a swipe at it, but cut down the Mayor's new curtains instead. He jabbed at the machine again, and the Mayor's wife shot up the rest of the way to the ceiling, shook down a yard of plaster and came down with a wallop, complete with machine and some of the wall.

Commander Hardaport, hard at rescuing Miss Frenzie, managed to get the Professor's Zipper to shoot up, but it took Miss Frenzie with it. The Commander shouted nautical commands and pressed buttons. Miss Frenzie came down again and shot up to the ceiling once more.

'Avast there!' shouted the Commander.

Miss Frenzie did three more ups and downs before the Commander managed to disentangle her from the machine and stop it with a sharp kick that hurt him more than it did the machine, as he wasn't wearing his sea boots.

The Professor was having trouble with the Vicar's wife who was still up against the ceiling. He fiddled with the machine. The Vicar's wife came down with a run on top of him. The Professor pressed the machine button and the Vicar's wife went sailing up

187

again accompanied by the Professor, whose coat had got caught in her zip.

All over Pagwell the Zipper Rescue Operations were going on. Firemen were failing to rescue schoolteachers; the Catapult Cavaliers were unsuccessful in rescuing librarians; hospital orderlies had no chance of rescuing non-librarians, and police-men were being arrested by bad-tempered zipping machines and imprisoned on ceilings accompanied by ladies they hardly knew.

But at last it was over. The Professor's machines were subdued, busted-up, collapsed or otherwise dealt with. Ginnibag & Knitwoddle did a roaring trade in button-down-the-front dresses from zipper-allergic ladies, while other ladies made up their minds to make do with wire coat-hangers suitably manipulated to zip themselves up and down in comparative safety.

But the Professor's Zipper produced one happy ending. A young policeman got married to a rather attractive girl librarian, whom he'd met in the zipper when they got fixed together, and he had proposed to her on the seventeenth trip up to the ceiling.

From *Professor Branestawm's Perilous Pudding*

Solution to Professor Branestawm's Dictionary Quiz
1I, 2C, 3H, 4F, 5D, 6J, 7E, 8B, 9A, 10G

Mrs Flittersnoop
Asks for a Rise

When Mrs Flittersnoop asked Professor Branestawm for an increase in wages because of the high cost of living, how did Professor Branestawm prove to her that she didn't really work at all?

'Well, um, er, ah,' he said, looking at her over his spectacles. 'There are three hundred and sixty-five days in the year, are there not?'

'Yes, indeed, I'm sure, sir,' agreed Mrs Flittersnoop.

'But', said the Professor, 'you work for eight hours a day only, out of the twenty-four. So you work only one third of the three hundred and sixty-five days, which is, shall we say, a hundred and twenty-two days.'

'Well, yes, I suppose so, if you say so, sir,' said Mrs Flittersnoop.

'Then,' went on the Professor, 'you do not work on Sundays, of course, so that makes fifty-two days to take away from the hundred and twenty-two, leaving seventy days. But then you always have another day off each week, which I, um, ah, agree you deserve, so that leaves only eighteen days.'

'Lawks a mussy me!' said Mrs Flittersnoop.

'And you have a fortnight's holiday,' said the Professor, 'and fourteen days from the remaining eighteen leaves only four days,'

'Oh, dear,' said Mrs Flittersnoop.

'And those four days are Good Friday, Easter Monday, Christmas Day and Boxing Day,' said the Professor. 'So you see, you really do not do any work at all,'

'Well, indeed, yes, I'm sure, sir,' said Mrs Flittersnoop, whose head had begun to go round and round just as Colonel Dedshott did when the Professor explained things. 'It really makes you wonder how all the work gets done, sir.'

'Yes, doesn't it?' said the Professor. But he gave her the increase in wages just the same because he knew she deserved it.

From *Professor Branestawm's Compendium*

To Please
Mrs Flittersnoop

Mrs Flittersnoop was never a one to complain, as she would have told you herself. In fact, she had been telling the Professor so for weeks and weeks.

No, Mrs Flittersnoop was never a one to complain. 'But really, sir, if I might make so bold as to say so,' she said, 'what with this hot weather and the extra rooms that have been built on to the house, and your new inventory on the roof, sir, not to mention the way people do take to popping in to see you at all hours, I'm not saying that I couldn't do with a bit of help now and then.'

'Oh, ah, um, yes of course!' said the Professor, closing all his five pairs of spectacles together with a rattle. 'Of course. Your sister from Lower Pagwell, Mrs Flittersnoop. By all means, or if the apex of the triangle ABC bisect the line DE with a temperature of . . .'

'It wasn't my sister Aggie I was thinking of, thank you all the same, I'm sure,' said Mrs Flittersnoop, dropping a tea-tray rather clangishly to stop the Professor going off into scientific thoughts again.

'Um, a, ah, I see!' said the Professor, who didn't see at all. 'You have another cousin, perhaps, or an auntie. Ask them up by all means.'

'Thank you, sir, but it's these labour-saving things I was thinking of, sir, if you don't mind my saying so. They do bring out some wonderful machines for letting you go to the pictures on washing-day, or so the advertisements say. Not that you can believe all they tell you in advertisements and not that I was ever much of a one for the pictures, but . . .'

She got no farther. The word machines had set the Professor off in the most non-stoppable way.

'Um, ah, yes, machines, let me see,' he said. 'What sort of machines? To do what sort of things? How about a machine for making cups of tea?' He was three parts of the way through an explanation of his idea of a machine like that, with numbered buttons to press according to how many lumps of sugar you took, and a lever to pull if you wanted China tea, when Mrs Flittersnoop managed to stop him and do a bit of explaining herself, which made the Professor's head go round for a change.

At last, after some very mixed up sort of conversation and plenty of waving of hands and a great deal of domestic-sounding talk from Mrs Flittersnoop and no end of scientific sort of exclamations from the Professor, they managed to decide how many hoped-to-be-labour-saving inventions could be done with about the house. Then the Professor went into his inventory to start inventing and Mrs Flittersnoop went down to her sister Aggie at Lower Pagwell, partly to tell her all about things and partly to get out of the way in case the Professor's inventing caused any drastic, sensational or collapsible kinds of uproar, which it was rather probably likely to do.

For weeks and weeks the Professor stayed in his inventory, only popping out now and then to say, 'Mrs Flittersnoop, have you seen the small screwdriver?' and 'Mrs Flittersnoop, will you go out and get me some long nails,' and 'Mrs Flittersnoop, come and show me what goes on the table first when you lay tea,' and 'Mrs Flittersnoop, can you hold this while I fix a spring to it?'

The first few times there was no reply, because Mrs Flittersnoop was still at her sister Aggie's, where she'd finished telling her about the Professor and was being told about her sister Aggie's little girl's hair that wouldn't go curly, not though they put it in papers every night and gave her burnt crusts for breakfast every morning. But after a bit Mrs Flittersnoop began to think she'd rather be possibly blown to bits over the Professor's inventions than absolutely certainly talked to bits over her sister Aggie's little girl's uncurlable hair. So she went back just in time to see the small screwdriver being run away with by the next-door cat. Then she got things, and showed him this and that, and held one thing and another. And she took the Professor his meals into his inventory, as he couldn't stop to come out for them, and several times he invented them into his inventions instead of eating them.

Then one frantic Friday, when the baker left a large brown loaf instead of a small one, and the milkman didn't come the second time, and the laundry sent back one of the best tablecloths with a teeny hole in it marked round with a terrific circle of red cotton, which was their way of saying they hadn't done it – the Professor came bursting out of his inventory with pairs of spectacles hung precariously on all parts of him and his mouth full of screws.

'Success! Magnificent success!' cried the Professor, trying to put a handful of screws on his nose in mistake for one of his pairs of spectacles and letting them trickle down all over his face. 'Mrs Flittersnoop, I have altered all our ideas of housework. My inventions will make housekeeping a game. I will demonstrate them to you.'

'Indeed, sir, that's very good, I'm sure,' said Mrs Flittersnoop, who felt that her ideas of housekeeping could do with some altering and who found housekeeping for the Professor rather a game as it was.

'There you are,' said the Professor proudly. He pointed to a row of the most uncalled-for-looking arrangements. They were his housework-doing machines, and they consisted of:

1. A washing-up Machine with detachable soap shaker and a knob which, when twiddled, caused the machine to put away the crockery it had just washed up.

2. A Bed-making Machine adjustable for single and double beds and complete with pillow-

case putting-on gear.

3. A Window-cleaning Machine, arranged to crawl up the walls to do the outsides and wipe its wheels carefully on the mat before coming in to do the insides.

4. A Ceiling Dusting Machine, with rotary cobweb eradicator.

5. A table-laying Machine, fitted with different coloured buttons to be pressed according to what meal was to be laid. (The Professor was determined to have coloured buttons on something.) It had a special lever for Breakfast-in-bed. This machine could also be reversed for clearing away again after meals.

6. A Stair-rod Polishing Machine.

7. A Fire-laying-and-lighting Machine, with automatic coal smasher, coke buster, oscillating poker and cinder disposer.

8. A Floor-polishing Machine, with rug-shaking attachment fitted with a string to be wound-up or let-out according to the pattern of the rug to be shaken.

There was also a detector for finding out where the marmalade had been put, as Mrs Flittersnoop often put it in different places, and a highly elaborate and nowhere near understandable device for making used matches strikable again.

'Well, I do think that's nice, that I do, sir,' said Mrs Flittersnoop. She very gingerly tried the Washing-up Machine on the dinner things. *Zim-zim-zim, clankety splosh whiz-whir.* All done!

'There now,' she cried, and turned on the Table-laying Machine with the 'Tea' button pressed. *Popetty-pip, swish, clink, tinkle.* Tea laid!

'Well, I never, that I'm sure, sir!' she exclaimed, coming over all delighted.

'Look at this one,' shouted the Professor from upstairs, where he'd unmade the beds and made them again ten times with his machine.

The machines were most successful. All except the Marmalade Detector, which would keep finding the lemon curd and the apricot jam instead, possibly as they were something like the same colour. But what was that to worry one, with all the housework getting itself done, *clankety-poppety-chug-a-chug-zim?* What indeed? The Professor's house resounded with mechanical noises. Everywhere shone and sparkled. The place was almost uncomfortably clean. The meals were ready with slightly troublesome regularity because the Professor hardly ever managed to be ready for a meal at the exact moment that Mrs Flittersnoop and the machines had it ready for him. The windows were so clean that people living two streets away could almost see the pattern on the wallpaper. The stair rods glittered. The toast rack was completely crumbless. You could have eaten off the ceiling if it hadn't been too much of an upside-down thing to do. And as for the floors, they were most drastically hygienic.

Professor Branestawm went round to his friend, Colonel Dedshott of the Catapult Cavaliers, to tell him about the machines and he made the Colonel's head go round and round so rapidly, explaining everything at once, that he had to put his hat on even though he was indoors.

'I must make you some machines, Dedshott,' said the Professor. 'You'll be surprised. Alter all your ideas of housework. They will make housekeeping a game,' he said.

'Ha, very clever, Branestawm, you know, what!' said the Colonel, whose idea of housework was to let his two ex-Catapult Cavaliers Butlers do it by numbers. 'No use to me, though. Not enough work here. Manage very well, what! House clean as new pin, dash it!'

'Um!' grunted the Professor. 'Well, what about a cup of tea?'

And as he said the words a cup and saucer landed in the front garden and smashed to bits on a pink stone rabbit the Colonel's step-cousin had given him.

'Good gracious!' cried the Professor. 'That looks like one of my cups and saucers. I recognize the pattern. Doesn't match. Invented it myself,' He dashed out just in time to catch a sugar basin, while the Colonel following close behind received a bread-and-butter plate on the head and a milk jug on his foot.

'Table-laying Machine!' gasped the Professor. 'Or else Washing-up Machine! Control spring must have slipped!'

Crockery was falling in showers in the streets of Great Pagwell as the Professor, still holding the basin into which his spectacles were falling as he ran, followed by Colonel Dedshott with half a bread-and-butter plate lodged on his very military hat, tore round to the Professor's house, from the windows of which the crockery was being hurled.

'You take front, I'll take rear!' panted the Colonel, coming over rather strategic. The house was more than ever full of automatic noises. But it was no longer even comfortably clean. Everywhere was patent-pandemonium and ultra-uproar and mechanical-muddle.

'Oh dear, good gracious me!' wailed the Professor, dodging a large rug that came hurtling downstairs, wrapped round three-dozen stair rods. 'Mrs Flitter-snoop! Mrs Flittersnoop!'

But Mrs Flittersnoop was at the pictures. Lucky for her, perhaps.

Crash! Eight glass tumblers, full of coke, were slammed down on the dining-room table and immediately snatched up again and washed in stair-rod polish.

'Help, oh dear, help!' cried the Professor. 'Machines have got mixed up.'

They certainly had. Each machine was trying to do bits of the other machines' jobs. The Floor-polishing and Rug-shaking Machine had shaken the tea-table cloth so vigorously that all the tea-things had gone flying out of the window. The Washing-up Machine had already taken the windows out, washed and dried them, and put them in the china-cupboard. The Table-laying Machine, with all its buttons pressed through hitting the door, was doing its best to lay breakfast, dinner, tea and supper all at once, using windows instead of crockery and sheets instead of table-cloths. The Fire-lighting Machine had got itself made into the Professor's bed and was filling the pillows with coal. The Marmalade Detector was triumphantly waving about a pot of marmalade it had managed to find at last and the marmalade was flying up and sticking to the ceiling. Which was giving the Ceiling-dusting Machine a time of it, as marmalade is so much less dust-away-able than cobwebs.

'All right, Branestawm!' shouted Colonel Dedshott, climbing through the scullery window, where he was promptly seized and washed up very thoroughly by the Window-cleaning Machine assisted by the Floor-polishing Machine.

'Pah, dash it, you know,' he spluttered, managing to push the Window-cleaning Machine into the kitchen fireplace, where it began to sweep the chimney with a wash-leather. 'Confound your inventions, Branestawm. Look at me!'

But the Professor couldn't look at anyone. He was completely enveloped in four tablecloths, two eiderdowns, and a yard and a half of stair carpet with the Ceiling-dusting Machine, which had given up the marmalade as a bad job, on top of him, busily making used matches strikable and putting them in the toast rack.

With grunts and growls the Colonel got the Professor untangled just as four of the machines began a twisted-together and inside-out sort of bed-making on the stairs with three rugs, a teapot, an old coat of Mrs Flittersnoop's, a yesterday's currant cake, and seven roller-towels, while the Marmalade Detector, having used up all the marmalade on the ceiling, was rapidly sprinkling honey, golden syrup and yellow plum jam over the bathroom

'Oh, my goodness! Oh, good gracious! Oh, bless me, why do I keep inventing things like this?' spluttered the Professor.

Mrs Flittersnoop came back from the pictures, gave one look and three screams, and went back to her sister Aggie's. *Bang, thud, zim-a-zim, splosh!* 'Bless me!' *Poppety-slam.* 'Confound the thing, what!' *Ziz-ziz-clank.* 'Pah!' *Wow!*

The Professor managed to twiddle some knobs and pull some levers which put the Window-cleaning and Ceiling-dusting Machines out of action. Gradually he got the upper hand. Gradually the mechanical tumult died down.

The Colonel sank wearily on to the Professor's bed and instantly had his pockets filled with coal by the Fire-lighting Machine that was still there.

At last all the machines were either stopped or smashed or otherwise dealt with and the Professor and the Colonel went to the Colonel's house for plenty of hot baths, and the Professor put on an old uniform of the Colonel's while his own clothes were cleaned, but didn't look any more rum than usual because it was impossible.

'My Housekeeping Machines are very clever, though I say it myself,' said the Professor some time later, after Mrs Flittersnoop had had her sister Aggie and her cousin Kate and her Auntie Helen and her friend Frannie Fussfast along to help get the Professor's house un-mechanically cleaned up with quite unscientific brooms and brushes and mops. 'I have therefore presented them as an, er, as a special exhibit to West Pagwell Technical Institute Museum,' he went on, 'they should prove most instructive.'

That week, all the Pagwell newspapers printed photos of the machines with a little note under them, saying 'Quaint gardening implements discovered by Professor Ramskorn and presented by him to West Pagwell Museum.'

And Mrs Flittersnoop had to go on managing as best she could by having her sister Aggie up to give her a hand whenever she felt she needed it, which was often.

Thank goodness, Mrs Flittersnoop was never a one to complain.

From *Professor Branestawm's Treasure Hunt*

Table-Laying
Made Easy

Professor Branestawm's Table-laying machine was a disaster, but here is a nice simple way of setting the table ready for meals.

You'll have to get Mum's co-operation for this but once you explain the idea to her she'll probably be quite enthusiastic. She may even like it so much she'll reward you by letting you help with the washing-up.

You will need three trays and you arrange these as follows:

Tray Number 1 On this you put all the things you usually lay on the table for breakfast, but not the tea or coffee things.

Tray Number 2 Here you put everything you would normally put on the table for lunch or dinner. This means that if you have put salt and pepper on tray number 1, you'll need a second set of salt and pepper for tray number 2.

Tray Number 3 On this you put the cups and saucers, etc., that you will need for tea or coffee.

But where are you going to keep all these trays? Well, Mum will almost certainly be able to clear space on a shelf for them because she won't need so much room for all the assorted china and glass you have to clatter through at present to lay a meal. That old tea service with square poppies on it that Cousin May gave you, for instance, can go up on top of the cupboard with those cracked vases and the leaking kettle that you never use.

Now to work the system.

Whatever meal you want to lay, you simply get out tray number 1 or 2, and transfer the things from it to the table. When the meal is finished and the things washed up you put them back on their tray, instead of sorting them all out and putting the knives back among the spoons, and getting the plates in the

wrong pile, and trying to force the cornflakes packet in between the row of jars with hardly any jam in them that can't be washed up yet because it would be a shame to waste the jam.

And whenever you need tea or coffee, either by itself or with a meal, there is everything handy on tray number 3. This method, of course, does away with Professor Branestawm's Marmalade Detector as the marmalade is already on tray number 1 for breakfast. It may even make it possible for the family actually to sit down and eat breakfast instead of tearing up the road to the bus stop with bread and marmalade in one hand and a satchel in the other.

From *Professor Branestawm's Do-It-Yourself Handbook*

The Pipes of Pandemonium

'It isn't as loud this time,' said Mrs Flittersnoop. 'No,' said the Professor, 'but it's going on longer.'

'But not so long as last Thursday,' said Mrs Flittersnoop.

'Friday mornings are the worst,' said the Professor. 'We shall have to get something done about it.' He gathered up his five pairs of spectacles and went into his study, dropping three of them into the waste-paper basket.

They had been talking about water pipe noises.

'I do hope we aren't going to have all that trouble we had some time ago,' said Mrs Flittersnoop, following him into his study and fishing the spectacles out of the waste-paper basket. 'The noise was so awful we couldn't sleep for it, and then when it stopped we couldn't sleep without it because we'd got so used to it.'

'Ah yes,' said the Professor, 'I remember. I had to invent a noise-making machine so that we could sleep, and gradually make it less noisy. But I'm not going to do that again. I shall call in the plumbers.'

'You aren't going to have a try at it yourself first?' asked Mrs Flittersnoop, hoping that he wasn't.

But she needn't have worried, because the Professor was deep in special inventions for car parks that could put in subways under roundabouts, and thus park your car and cross the road at the same time.

He wrote to some plumbers that he knew and asked them to come and deal with the pipes. They came, two of them, a short, jolly little man in a cap and a very young man with a lot of hair.

'The pipes go *weeeeee*, when the hot tap is turned on,' said the Professor.

'And they go *Zim, Zim, Zim, Zim*, when the cold tap is turned off,' added Mrs Flittersnoop.

'If the hot tape is turned off very slowly,' said the Professor, 'the noise goes on, and if the cold tap is turned on very suddenly, the noise then stops. But if both taps are turned on at once and then turned off separately, the noise stops, then goes on again, until the hot water tap is turned on and the cold tap is turned on and then off, and then the noises stop, start again and stop. Unless of course the cold tap is turned on first and both taps are turned off together.'

'Ah!' said long hair.

'You gotta be re-piped,' said the jolly man, grinning like a Prime Minister.

'I gotta be what did you say?' asked the Professor,

thinking his ears weren't working properly.

'Re-piped, guv,' said the jolly man. 'Them noises what your pipes are making, now that we can stop. That's just a hair lock.'

'A hair lock?' said the Professor. 'How can a lock of hair be responsible for all that noise?'

'Not an *air* lock, a *hair* lock,' said the jolly man.

'I think he means air lock,' said Mrs Flittersnoop, trying to be helpful.

'Yes, a hair lock in them pipes,' said the jolly man. 'We can sort that out easy, but all these water pipes are proper wore out, guv, and that's a fact.'

He reached under the sink, and pulled out a length of pipe which crumbled up in his hands.

'See what I mean!' said the jolly man.

'Um,' said long hair, taking half a cigarette from behind his left ear, looking at it and putting it behind his right ear.

'Oh dear, oh dear!' cried Mrs Flittersnoop. 'That sounds awful! Do you mean we must have all the water pipes taken out and new ones put in?'

'Throughout,' said the jolly man. 'Otherwise you'll get trouble.'

'We already have trouble,' said the Professor. 'We have trouble with the pipes making noises. Do I understand you to say that we must now have more trouble in order to get rid of the trouble we already have?'

'Well, it's like this, guv,' said the jolly man, popping a peppermint into his mouth and rattling it round his teeth. 'If we don't re-pipe you, the pipes what are rotten are liable to break up, and then where are you?'

'I'm, 'ere,' said long hair.

'Not you!' said the jolly man. 'I mean to say, guv, you could be flooded out proper.'

'How long will it take to re-pipe us?' asked the Professor.

'Well, not more'n two weeks, that is to say, two working weeks, which, as we only work five days a week and a full week is seven days, means fourteen days' work,' said the jolly man. 'And that comes out at about three weeks, give or take a few days. On the other hand, it might just take a couple of hours. You never can tell.'

'But we can't be without water for three weeks!' gasped Mrs Flittersnoop, thinking of all the washing she couldn't do. 'We should run out of the Professor's pyjamas!'

'Ah now, Mrs Flittersnoop,' said the Professor. 'You could go and stay with your sister Aggie I have no doubt.'

'Well, yes, indeed, I'm sure, sir, I could do that,' said Mrs Flittersnoop. 'But what about you?'

'I have an idea that this would be a good opportunity to go and stay with some friends of mine in Pagwell Gardens Suburb who asked me to visit them,' said the Professor.

So the jolly man and long hair were told to get on with the re-piping, and Professor Branestawm went to stay with Mr and Mrs Horace Hokkibats. They were a very sporting couple he had met at a lecture on table tennis in its relation to ludo under the continental influence of Italian basket-ball, which he had once attended by mistake.

Mr Hokkibats was a tall, skinny gentleman with square spectacles. He was a part-time sports commentator with the Pagwell Broadcasting Company, because he could talk extremely quickly and describe games even faster than people could play them. In fact, when he was commentating on a football game, the players had a hard job keeping up with him. The match of the year between Pagwell United and Pagwell Friday resulted in a score of Pagwell United 2, Pagwell Friday 3, and Horace Hokkibats 7.

Mrs Hetty Hokkibats, who was a retired games teacher, was small, round and bouncy, like a tennis ball. Both of them loved games of all kinds, and their house was rather like Wimbledon, Lords, Henley and the Imperial Chess Club, all in one building.

'I'm sure you'll find plenty to amuse you here, Professor,' said Hetty Hokkibats, lobbing the Professor's hat on to a netball goal in the hall. 'We are great believers in making life a game.'

'Rather!' said her husband. 'Well, we had better make an ascent on your room right away. Breakfast kick-off at eight thirty tomorrow.'

He carried the Professor's suitcase up the stairs with great difficulty, partly because the Professor had packed quantities of inventing tools in with his clothes, which made the case very heavy, and partly because the staircase was laid out as a bowling alley, where you bowled up the stairs at some skittles arranged on the first landing and your ball was returned down a chute at the side of the stairs.

'I hope you slept well, Professor,' said Mrs Hokkibats, next morning.

'I, um, er, that is to say,' mumbled the Professor. In fact, he had hardly slept at all because the ceiling of his bedroom was marked out as a chess problem, and he had been trying to work it out all night. In addition the bed was made like a dodgem car, and kept sliding round the room, bumping off the furniture. He had finally managed to get a little sleep by sitting in the wardrobe.

Mrs Hokkibats blew a sharp blast on a whistle, and Mr Hokkibats, who had been limbering up on the lawn, came running into the dining-room and breakfast began.

'And it's bacon coming down on the left side, closely followed by fried eggs, but dry toast looks like overtaking if kippers don't catch them at the first fork,' jabbered Mr Hokkibats, as Mrs Hokkibats dealt plates of breakfast round like playing cards in a mad game of whist.

The dining-table was a table tennis table, so that you had to pass the salt and pepper and marmalade over the net. If you missed it, that counted against you, and you lost half an egg or a piece of toast.

'It's all over with the porridge, and the rice crispies are well down!' shrieked Horace. 'Now it's two to one the boiled eggs get cracked and don't make the cup.'

Mr Hokkibats neatly fielded a grilled kidney and sent the Professor down a fast leg-break sausage. The Professor, who rarely remembered to eat any breakfast anyway, would not even have tried now, except that Mrs Hokkibats failed to return the toast her husband had sent over in a half volley so that it landed on the Professor's plate and he ate it almost in his sleep.

'Well, we're coming to the end of another exciting breakfast!' said Mr Hokkibats. 'And it looks as though Mrs Hokkibats will shortly be relegated to the washing-up. In the meanwhile, Professor, I suggest I show you round our house.'

They looked at the bathroom, which had an enormous dart-board on the wall where you had to score double top before you could have a bath. The drawing-room was papered with crossword puzzles, which you had to rub out as soon as you had done them so that they would be ready for the next person to attempt. There was a clock golf in the hall, where you had to stand inside the grandfather clock and try to get the ball into the umbrella stand at the far end.

All the time they were looking Mr Hokkibats kept up a running commentary that would have won the eight million metres in the Olympic Games, explaining it all to the Professor, who couldn't listen fast enough.

'Um, most remarkable,' he said, wondering how he could invent some way of getting out of the place with out first having to throw a double six with dice, or draw the act of hearts from a pack of cards.

By the end of the afternoon, the Professor, tired out by playing games he didn't understand, decided to ring up his house to see how the re-piping was going. But somehow he managed to dial the wrong number; he thought he was connected to his own house, but he had got the Great Pagwell School of Scottish Music instead.

'Have you done the pipes at my house yet?' he asked, not realizing that anything was wrong.

'Is it pipes ye're wanting, then?' said a very Scottish lady at the other end. 'Weel, it isna Hogmanay nor Robbie Burrrns' birthday, ye ken, but if it's the pipes ye're wanting we'll no be stopping ye.'

'No, no, I'm Professor Branestawm,' protested the Professor. 'It's at my house, the pipes. Is everything in, um, ah, order?'

'Aye, I've got yer order, Professor, never fear,' said the Scottish lady. 'We'll be away and see to it the noo.'

She rang off, still thinking the Professor wanted bagpipes played at his home. And, with true Scottish efficiency, the Great Pagwell School of Scottish Music sent plenty of pipers and a' and a' round to the Professor's house.

Meanwhile Colonel Dedshott had decided to go and visit Professor Branestawm at the Hokkibats household.

'May be glad of a chat with no inventing to do. Probably a bit bored by now, what!' He mounted his horse and rode off.

Mr and Mrs Hokkibats welcomed him with open arms, and before he knew where he was the Colonel was involved in a complicated game of tennis on horseback, which he found rather difficult because his horse kept tripping over the croquet hoops on the tennis court.

Professor Branestawm saw his chance. He grabbed a bicycle belonging to Mr Hokkibats and set off for home as fast as he could, which wasn't very fast because the bicycle was a special one made for cycle racing in the drawing-room and no matter how hard you pedalled it barely moved.

'This is awful!' groaned the Professor. 'It would be quicker to walk.' He leant the bicycle against a lamp-post, and started walking. Then he found it would be even quicker to run and quicker still to take a bus.

At last he arrived at his house.

'Oh, no, this is worse than ever!' he cried.

The plumbers had gone, it was true. But the noise was worse than before.

Weeeee! Owowowowowo!

'I won't have it!' cried the Professor. 'I shall ring up the water company and complain about the plumbers.'

But of course it wasn't the plumbers' fault the noises were worse than ever. In every room of the Professor's house there were enormous persons in kilt, sporran, tartan and skene-dhu (which is a sort of Scottish flick knife used for stabbing wild haggis). And they were playing the bagpipes for all they were worth, which was a good deal, because Scottish people are very careful with their money.

Weee! Zooooom! Weee!

And, because they were all in different rooms, stamping up and down as bagpipers have to, they couldn't hear what the other were playing. So they were all playing different tunes. And the mixture of 'Flowers of the Forest' and 'Scotland the Brave' and

various other laments, marches and reels certainly sounded much worse than the water pipe noise.

'Stop this noise at once! I want to telephone!' shouted the Professor to the piper in the dining-room.

'What's that?' said the piper

'I want to telephone!' shouted the Professor.

'I canna hear ye for these damn pipes!' shouted the piper.

The Professor rushed upstairs.

'Yon's a queer mon,' said the piper to himself. 'He doesna like the pipes.'

The Professor went out into the garden, where he ran into Colonel Dedshott, who had managed to get away from the Hokkibatses at last by jumping over the tennis net on his horse and galloping off.

'My word, what's all this, by Jove?' he was saying, as he got off his horse.

'The Professor doesna like the pipes,' said the piper.

'My word, no, I should think not!' said the Colonel. 'If the water pipes in my house made that row I'd have something to say, I can tell you!'

He stamped into the house to look for the Professor and found him sitting on the floor at the foot of the stairs, shouting at the telephone.

'But we've stopped the noises, guv,' said the jolly man at the other end of the phone, because the Professor had got on to the plumbers instead of the water company, which he was trying to telephone. 'We got rid of that hair lock, and everything's nice and quiet, you'll find.'

'*Quiet?*' yelled the Professor.

Colonel Dedshott stumped up the stairs shouting military commands. Commander Hardaport, the Professor's next-door neighbour, came in shouting complaints, because the only kind of pipe he liked was a bosun's pipe. And the noise was worse than ever.

But fortunately at that moment Mrs Flittersnoop came back from her sister Aggie's and made tea and shortbread for the pipers. As soon as they noticed this they stopped piping immediately. Two very agile pipers did a sword dance on fish knives in the garden, for a lark. Colonel Dedshott exchanged English and Scottish military stories with the chief piper, who was very high up in a Highland regiment. And Commander Hardaport (Retired) told tall sea stories to the other pipers, who were also tall.

And the Professor sank into a chair, and said, 'Well, thank goodness that's over, whatever it was! And thank goodness the water pipe noises are finished with.'

But just then a wailing and gurgling broke out overhead as Mrs Flittersnoop turned the cold tap off rather quickly after re-filling the tea kettle.

'Stop it!' shouted the Professor. 'I will *not* have it! Fetch the plumbers! Call the water company!'

But it wasn't necessary to call any of these distinguished people. The chief piper, who was used to climbing about in the Highlands, climbed to the roof and found that what was causing the noises hadn't been the fault of the water pipes at all. It was an old invention of the Professor's for protecting the house against being struck by lightning. He had put it up in the roof and connected it to the water pipes for safety. And it made lightning-conducting noises which the water pipes transmitted right through the house.

That left the Professor to decide whether it was better to be protected against being struck by lightning during a storm than to be struck by water pipe noises all the time, unless you remembered to turn the hot water on first or the cold water off first, or to turn them off slowly or suddenly according to which you had turned on or off first.

From *Professor Branestawm's Great Revolution*

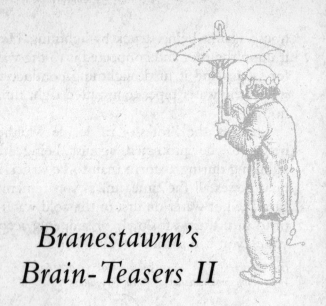

Branestawm's
Brain-Teasers II

Where should an astronaut stop?
At a parking meteor.

Why does a bad singer break into song?
Because he can't find the key.

When a bus stops, why do some of the passengers seem to be on fire?
Because you see them alight.

Why is a pop concert draughty?
Because of all the fans.

What do nuclear scientists eat for lunch?
Fission chips.

Where is the best place to hold a party on board ship?
Where the funnel be.

What goes tick-tick, bow-bow?
A watchdog.

Why do men get paid extra for working on top of Big Ben?
Because they're working overtime.

What dish does a policeman use when he apprehends someone?
Irish stew, in the name of the law (I arrest you).

From *Professor Branestawm's Compendium*

The Wild
Washing-Day

There now,' cried Mrs Flittersnoop in alarm, 'if it hasn't started to rain! I must get the washing in.'

'If it hasn't started to rain,' put in the Professor in his most helpful voice, 'you need not get the washing in until it does start.'

But Mrs Flittersnoop was already buried under sheets and pillowcases and pyjamas while the rain pattered happily down, making pretty noises which Mrs Flittersnoop was not prepared to appreciate.

'Um, ah, let me help,' cried the Professor, dashing forward gallantly and treading on the end of a sheet Mrs Flittersnoop was rather wrapped up in, which caused her to fall over and trip up the Professor. By the time they had got themselves sorted out and the washing safely indoors two things had happened. It had stopped raining and the washing was covered in muddy footmarks.

'I shall have to wash them again, that's all,' she cried, turning on the hot tap and getting out her extra large sized, bargain offer packet of Miracle Washing Powder that Gets Whites Whiter than White with 3p off recommended price.

Meanwhile, the sun had come out and it was a lovely day for drying the clothes Mrs Flittersnoop had just re-washed.

'Allow me to give you a hand with hanging them out,' said the Professor, when Mrs Flittersnoop emerged from the steam with the last washed sock.

There was a great deal of 'Be careful with my best blouse!' and 'Have you any more, um, ah, clothes pegs?' and 'Don't let that pillowcase drop on the grass!' and other washing conversation. The Professor managed to peg the shirt he was wearing on the line by mistake and Mrs Flittersnoop only just got him unpegged in time to prevent him from being hauled up with the rest of the washing.

'There now,' she said, when the last towel and final piece of teacloth was pegged out and the line hauled up. 'They'll soon be dry with this sun.'

But the very next moment some rain clouds blew up, down came a considerable amount of rain and they had to gather all the washing in again.

And by the time they had it safely inside the house, which took some doing as the Professor got himself entangled in a tablecloth, the sun had come out again and they had to hang the washing out once more.

Over at the vicarage there was a similar problem. Maisie and Daisie, the Vicar's twin daughters, were having a nice sunbathe in their new bikinis, both exactly alike, when the rain came down on them and they had to dash indoors before their false eyelashes started dissolving.

But they had no sooner got inside and started to put on some clothes when out came the sun and they had to strip off and rush out again.

Then before they could get toasted even a pale biscuit colour the rain came down and drove them in.

'It, ah, really seems to me,' gasped Professor Branestawm, after five more ins and outs with the washing, 'that we are managing to get the washing out when it is raining and inside when the sun is shining.'

'Yes, indeed, I'm sure, sir,' said Mrs Flittersnoop, who was wondering whether it wouldn't be quicker and easier to put the whole lot in the oven and bake them dry, but unfortunately she had a rather fierce fruit cake cooking and didn't dare open the oven door in case it went flop.

Professor Branestawm too was having a good think, which would probably turn out to be a bad think because it would almost certainly lead to a disastrously ingenious invention.

'The sun is now being used to warm people's houses,' he said to himself. 'Now if I can devise a way of using solar rays to operate an automatic, er, washing-line, it should be possible so to arrange, um, matters that the washing will be out in the garden when it is sunny and safely inside the house if it rains, instead of the other way about as we have been experiencing.'

Colonel Dedshott, who had just dropped in for a cup of tea, thought it was a jolly good idea, though he himself never bothered whether it was raining or not. His Catapult Cavaliers soldiers were quite used to getting soaking wet or boiling hot, and being in full marching order, piled up with everything but a colour television set and an aspidistra with the scorching sun beating down on them, or running about in little short pants and no vest, doing exercises, in an ice-cold, north-easterly wind. A soldier's life is very trying, but at least they always know they're going to get their pocket-money.

'There is already a method of heating houses by solar radiation,' said the Professor. 'All you have to do is take the roof off and replace it with solar panels. And if you can do that, why shouldn't I use the same principle to move the washing out into the garden while it is sunny?'

'Hum, ha, yes, by Jove!' grunted the Colonel, who didn't think there could be a military answer to that.

Just then the Vicar arrived, with his wife, to consult Mrs Flittersnoop about lemonade for the vicarage garden party, and the Professor started to tell the Vicar about his solar radiation-operated washing-line.

'Well, I suppose it would be all right,' murmured the Vicar, who felt that he ought to feel it was a bit un-Christian harnessing the sun to warm houses, but then you had to have progress, didn't you?

'I think it's a positively marvellous idea!' said the

Vicar's wife, having got the lemonade organized with Mrs Flittersnoop. 'I'm always having to rush out and get the washing in because it comes on to rain. My husband, of course, prays for a fine washing-day but we don't always get the right answer.'

So the Professor disappeared into his inventory and began the task of inventing an invention that would make sure the washing was in the garden when the sun was out and inside the house when it wasn't. And meanwhile Maisie and Daisie solved their problem by buying themselves a jar of some cream with a very expensive smell that was highly recommended by the advertisements for giving ladies a lovely sun tan without having to go out in the sun at all. Unfortunately it brought Masie and Daisie out in spots and they had to go and buy more jars of special ointment for hiding spots.

Professor Branestawm's world-shaking invention for keeping the washing in the sun took him a bit of time because he kept getting his molecules mixed up with his atoms, and at first his attempts at controlling solar radiation for drying clothes only made his tea get cold because he forgot to drink it. But at last the first sun-operated automatic washing-line in the world was ready to astonish the neighbours.

'Queer-looking craft,' said Commander Hard-aport (Retired). 'Never seen a rig like it in me life.'

'Ah, that is because you are looking at the bare framework,' said the Professor. 'When it is covered with washing you will find it more, ah, recognizable.'

Mrs Flittersnoop brought out the week's wash

and, in spite of the Professor giving her a helping hand, she actually managed to get it all arranged on the arms and lines of the machine, where it looked rather like something left over from the Spanish Armada.

The Vicar's wife, who had brought her washing along to have it done, sort of for charity while the demonstration was on, arranged the Vicar's pyjamas and surplices tastefully alongside the vicarage tablecloths. By this time the Professor's special washing-line had all sails set and was straining at its moorings.

'Ha!' exclaimed the Commander, a nautical gleam flickering in his eyes. 'Got your mizzen tops'ls under your t'gallants I see and your spinnakers are abaft your royals. Most unseaman-like. Never make a passage like that, y'know.'

But the Professor's sun-operated washing wasn't going to be put off course by naval talk from a next-door neighbour. As the sun came out it emitted a whirring sound like a cuckoo clock going backwards. Mrs Flittersnoop's best nightdress spread out, tablecloths flapped and the whole thing went gliding into the garden, sweeping Colonel Dedshott into a wheelbarrow and finally coming to rest on the calceolaria bed.

'Well, indeed I'm sure, I never, sir,' exclaimed Mrs Flittersnoop.

'The, er, washing will now remain out in the garden as long as the sun shines,' explained the Professor. 'But if it should come on to rain my invention will bring it all safely indoors out of the wet.'

'Pity we can't make it rain so as to see it do it,' said the Commander.

'Can't you make it rain for us, Professor?' asked Mr Stinckz-Bernagh, the science master from Pagwell College who had come to see what scientifically controlled laundry looked like. 'You did it once with a weather machine, I remember.'

But the Professor wasn't going to muck about with the weather any more. He had had enough of mauve snow mixed up with heat waves.

Just then Mr Marmaduke Mushington Mobley, who lived next door to the Professor on the other side from Commander Hardaport, turned on the hose to water his garden and a spray or two fell on the washing. Instantly the sun-operated clothes-line went about and tacked briskly back into the house, which would have taken the wind right out of Commander Hardaport's sails if he had had them with him.

'Goodness me, indeed, sir!' cried Mrs Flittersnoop, just getting out of the way before the washing-line could clap her best nightdress on her, which she thought would have been rather indelicate with so many gentlemen present.

Mr Marmaduke Mushington Mobley next door had got his hose under control now and was spraying his moon daisies, and so the washing-line went sailing out again into the sun under full canvas and hove to beside the sweet peas. But when Mr Marmaduke Mushington Mobley finished spraying his moon daisies and rushed across the garden to water his roses, another shower of water accidentally fell on the washing. The Professor's machine conscientiously sailed back indoors and promptly sailed out again.

Then what must happen but some real, genuine, wet rain came splashing down and the Professor's wonderful washing-line put its helm over and shot back inside the house, where it sailed into the dining-room and moored alongside the sideboard.

'Stop it! Stop it!' cried Mrs Flittersnoop. I've only just cleaned the silver.'

But the machine wasn't interested in silver, whether just cleaned or not. It disembarked most of the washing all over the room. The top of the Vicar's pyjamas was seated at the dining-table along with the Professor's shirts and Mrs Flittersnoop's best drip-dry blouses, where they seemed to be waiting for tea to be served.

'I, er, fear these sudden changes in the, um, ah, apparent weather have disturbed the rather delicate balance of the solar panel control units,' cried the Professor. He tried to get the washing back on the machine but the Vicar's pyjamas obviously weren't going to get up from the table till they had had their tea.

''Vast heaving!' cried Commander Hardaport (Retired), waving a telescope at the machine, which took it away from him, pegged it on one of its lines and shot out into the garden again as the sun had come out.

Meantime Maisie and Daisie had tried another kind of sun-tan cream but this turned them pale green and made them look as if they were made of marzipan.

'Let's go and ask Professor Branestawm to invent something to give us a nice tan while we stay indoors and play records,' said either Maisie or Daisie.

'Great!' cried Daisie or Maisie.

They arrived at the Professor's just in time to be scooped up by the washing-line and pegged out alongside the rock garden.

'Oh my goodness, my daughters!' wailed the Vicar's wife, while the Vicar sent up a hurried barrage of hopeful prayers and rushed to the rescue, accompanied by Colonel Dedshott and Commander Hardaport, uttering military and naval exclamations.

'Help!' cried Maisie and Daisie, both in the same kind of voice.

The machine dodged the rescuers and beat hurriedly to port among the gooseberry bushes.

'*Ow!*' cried Maisie (or was it Daisie?). 'I've heard that old story about being found under a gooseberry bush but I don't want to be sent back there.'

Colonel Dedshott took a swipe at the machine with his sword and cut the tops off two gooseberry bushes and the legs off the Vicar's pyjamas.

The machine gybed, went about and shot round to the front of the house, down the garden path and out into the road just as a van from the Great Pagwell Laundry came along.

Bong! Crash! Wallop, bing, tinkle, tinkle! The laundry van hit the washing-line machine amidships. The air was full of accident noises and laundry sounds. The Professor, Colonel Dedshott and the Vicar came tearing up yelling advice and warnings.

But the Laundry Man was a very dedicated

washing collector. He was out to collect washing and here was washing that needed collecting, so he bundled it all into his van and drove off. His van was a plentifully robust one and had hardly suffered at all in the crash except for some of the painted letters being scraped off, so that the name on the van read *Great Pagwell La dry*, which made it sound rather like a French sort of laundry.

But the Professor's incredible, mechanical, sun-operated washing-line had had it, three times over. Nothing was left but an awful lot of clothes-line and a great many bits of assorted metal.

'Oh, the washing!' cried Mrs Flittersnoop.

'My husband's pyjamas!' moaned the Vicar's wife.

But it was all right because the Great Pagwell Laundry were frightfully efficient and managed to return nearly all the washing to its rightful owners, carefully re-washed and dried indoors out of the rain. Only one pair of the Vicar's pyjamas went astray and that landed up at an Oxfam shop.

And Mrs Flittersnoop felt just a little bit relieved that she could now hang the washing out on a nice simple, innocent, inoffensive washing-line that wouldn't answer back. But being a very careful lady, she now hung it out to dry indoors to be on the safe side. Unless of course, the weather forecast said it was going to rain, and then she hung it out in the garden knowing they were due for a fine, sunny day.

From *Professor Branestawm Round the Bend*

*For the astounding revelation
that fills a long-felt want
in every household*

Read on . . .

Professor Branestawm's Incredible Discovery

HOW TO PUT TOOTHPASTE BACK INTO THE TUBE

It has been left to the genius of Professor Branestawm to discover how this domestic problem can be overcome without trouble or difficulty, without special machinery and without adding anything to the electric light bill.

Now, when you have squeezed out too much toothpaste, as you always do, you can put it back in the tube quite easily and so save the nation endless expense in wasted toothpaste.

HOW TO DO IT

To get toothpaste back into the tube, simply open the bottom the tube by unfolding the folded-over part. If you go on unfolding long enough you will find the tube opens right out. Put the toothpaste back in with a disused mustard spoon or the wrong end of a teaspoon. Then fold the end of the tube up again.

If Professor Branestawm doesn't get a knighthood for this it will not be the fault of Great Pagwell Council. They confidently expect the Prime Minister to declare a public holiday to celebrate this great discovery of the Professor's.

From *Professor Branestawm's Do-It-Yourself Handbook*

The Too-Many Professors

'L or' bless my heart, whatever can that awful smell be?' gasped Mrs Flittersnoop, coming out of the kitchen all of a dither, with a smudge of flour on her nose because she was making cakes and her hair all over the place because she was making haste. 'Can't be the drains, for the man was here only yesterday to see to them. Can't be something gone bad, for I turned out the larder with my own hands this very morning.'

Sniff, sniff, pw-o-o-ugh. It certainly was an extreme sort of smell. Much worse than drains, not so bearable as something gone bad, utterly unlike any kind of smell anyone has ever smelt.

'It's the Professor, I'll be bound,' said Mrs Flittersnoop, wiping her hands on her apron.

And it certainly was the Professor, for before Mrs Flittersnoop had time to get to the door of his inventory out he burst with a little bottle in one hand, a garden syringe in the other, and his clothes stained all the colours of the rainbow and some more besides.

'Amazing! Astounding!' he shouted, pushing Mrs Flittersnoop aside, dashing into his study and then coming back to fetch her in as well.

'Begging your pardon, sir, but if it's illegible spirits you're making I must give notice,' she said, putting her hands on her hips where they slipped off again because she was a bit thinnish.

'Listen,' gasped the Professor getting his five pairs of spectacles so mixed up that he could see four Mrs Flittersnoops all different sizes and one upside down. 'World will resound with discovery. Name a household word. Branestawm's bewildering bacteria, the secret of life revealed! I never used to think I was as clever as I thought I was, but now I see I'm much cleverer than I dared to hope I might be.'

Mrs Flittersnoop didn't answer. The Professor had just uncorked the bottle and the simply awful smellish odour immediately became so bad she had to bury her nose in her apron which unfortunately only buried half of it, because it was a long nose and a short apron.

'This liquid', said the Professor, all of a tremble with excitement, 'will bring to life any picture to which it is applied. Look at this.'

He poured some of the sparkling liquid into a glass jar, drew some up in the syringe and squirted it over a picture of some apples on the cover of a book. Nothing happened, except that the picture got wet.

'Very good, sir, I'm sure,' said Mrs Flittersnoop in a muffled sort of voice from inside the apron. 'And now I must be getting back to my cakes.' She was out of the room and half-way to the kitchen before the Professor could stop her and drag her back.

'Wait, wait, wait, wait!' he shouted excitedly. 'It takes time. Look, look!' he pointed with a quivering finger at the picture.

'Oo-er,' said Mrs Flittersnoop. 'It's going all lumpy like.'

It certainly was. The apples began to swell up, the picture went all nobbly. Green smoke rose from the paper. The smell would have got worse only it couldn't. Then suddenly four lovely rosy apples rolled out of the picture on to to the table, as real and solid as you please.

'Oh my!' exclaimed Mrs Flittersnoop.

'Try one,' said the Professor, and together they munched the apples. And except for a rather papery flavour and a funny feeling they gave you as if you were eating an apple in a dream that wasn't there at all but only seemed to be, the apples were certainly a success.

'It is rather a pity,' said the Professor, spraying a picture of a box of chocolates to life, 'that it costs more to make the liquid for doing this than it would cost to buy the things.'

'You don't say!' said Mrs Flittersnoop, taking a handful of the chocolates and not bothering about her cakes any more, which had burned themselves into cinders in the meantime, only neither of them could smell them because of the other smell, and thinking the Professor could just spray a few cakes out of a book if he wanted them.

'Yes,' said the Professor, hunting about among his books and papers, 'and there are certain limitations to the power of the liquid. The things it brings to life go back as they were when the liquid dries off.'

'Oo-er,' said Mrs Flittersnoop, thinking of the apples and chocolates she had eaten. But the Professor was pulling out a book with a picture of a cat in it.

'Let me try this,' he said. 'I don't know yet whether it will work with animals or people.'

He filled the syringe again while Mrs Flittersnoop hid behind the door in case the cat was a scratchy sort of one, which it was quite likely to be, because most of the Professor's books were about wildish kinds of animals.

Phiz-z-z-z, went the spray. They waited, the paper bulged, the picture smoked, the smell didn't get worse, just as before. Then – *Meow!* – out jumped the cat.

But oh good gracious and heavens above, the next minute with a terrific *whoosh* of a zoom the whole room was full of an elephant!

'Amazing!' gasped the Professor, struggling out of the waste-paper basket where the elephant had knocked him. But Mrs Flittersnoop slammed the door and rushed screaming all the way to her sister Aggie's in Lower Pagwell without even stopping to wipe the flour off her nose.

The cat jumped out of the window and followed her, still meowing because the picture of it had showed it meowing and it didn't seem to be able to stop. But most definitely awkward of all, the elephant squeezed its big self through the french windows and followed her too.

'Heavens!' gasped the Professor, getting so worked up that his socks came down. And he dashed after the elephant, dropping his glasses all over the place and holding his handkerchief hoping to be able to catch it and dry the wonderful liquid off it and make it go back into a picture, but not hoping so very much.

But while the Professor was chasing the elephant who was running after the cat who seemed to want to catch up with Mrs Flittersnoop, who definitely did want to get to her sister Aggie's, the most absolute things were going on in the Professor's room. Voices could have been heard if there had been anyone about to hear them. Rumblings and rustlings were occurring. Chatterings went up. People started talking round the place like goodness knows what.

When the elephant had come out of the picture so suddenly he'd upset the jar of wonderful liquid all over the Professor's photograph album. Good gracious, what a thing to do! Liquid that could make things come to life and all! And upset on a photograph album of all places!

When the Professor, who had given up the chase at Pagwell Gardens, came staggering back all out of breath the first thing he noticed was himself opening the door to himself.

'Good afternoon,' said the Professor, not recognizing himself.

'Don't take it for a moment, the sun's in my eyes,' said the other one of him.

The Professor was just wondering what the answer to that was when two more of himself, one at sixteen and one at twenty-two came out of the study, followed by three of Mrs Flittersnoop in different hats of her sister Aggie's, two of Colonel Dedshott, one before he joined the Catapult Cavaliers and one just after.

'Heavens!' cried the Professor. Pushing past them he dashed up the stairs, nearly falling over three more of himself aged eighteen months, cannoned into another Mrs Flittersnoop at fifteen, in fancy dress as Bo-Peep, on the landing. Feverishly he searched the rooms. Everywhere were more and more of himself, at all ages and in all sorts of clothes including one of him extra-specially young with nothing on at all but a big smile.

EVERYWHERE WERE MORE OF HIMSELF.

WITH NOTHING ON AT ALL
BUT A BIG SMILE·

Everywhere there were duplicate Mrs Flittersnoops and spare Colonel Dedshotts and extra copies of various friends and relations. The wonderful liquid had brought every single one of the photographs in the album to life. And they were all saying the same things over and over again.

'Don't take it yet, I've got the sun in my eyes,' and 'Had I better take my hat off first?' and 'Hurry up and take it, I must go in and get tea,' said 'I say, what a ripping camera!' and 'Baby want petty sing,' and 'Goo goo.' All of them were saying whatever they were saying when the photograph was taken and couldn't say anything else. But as they were all saying it together it began to get awful. Worst of all, there was half of a policeman who had got taken in one of the photos by mistake, and he kept hopping about on his one leg saying in a half sort of voice 'Pass along p ...' which was all he could manage of 'Pass along please.'

'Terrible! Terrible!' gasped the Professor, guessing what had happened although he hadn't any of his pairs of spectacles on and everyone looked a bit hazy, especially one of Mrs Flittersnoop that had been taken out of focus and was all hazy anyway and kept saying, 'Ploof woo woo muffn plith a woogle,' because of course her voice was out of focus too.

'Oh dear,' gasped the Professor, 'supposing I get mixed up with all these come-to-life-photo sort of people and forget which is really me?'

Just then there was a loud bang from the inventory where one of the Professors, aged sixteen, had been fiddling about trying to invent something and done an explosion instead.

Out dashed the Professor nearly in time to be hit by a piece of roof. But immediately a *rumblety bump* followed by loud wowing from inside the house made him dash back. Three of them, age eighteen months, had fallen down the stairs together. A thing he had done himself just after those particular photographs were taken.

'Ploof woo woo muffn plith a woogle,' shouted the out-of-focus hazy Mrs Flittersnoop rushing down the stairs. 'Pass along p . . . Pass along p . . . Pass along p . . .' cried the half policeman hopping along from the kitchen where he had been trying to eat half a pie he had found.

Then *pr-r-r-ing-g* went the door-bell and in came the real Colonel Dedshott.

'Ha! Hullo, Branestawm!' he said to one of the photo Professors, aged twenty or so. 'Party on and all that, what! Sorry to intrude, you know.'

'Hold it perfectly still while you press the lever,' said the photo Professor, who had been telling someone how to take the photo.

'Ha, ha! Yes, of course,' said the Colonel, not

understanding a bit of course but thinking the Professor was talking some of his professorish stuff which he wouldn't have understood anyway. 'Been for a holiday? You're looking well, 'pon my word you look ten years younger.'

'Hold it perfectly still while you press the lever,' retorted the photo Professor, who of course looked very much more than ten years younger than the real Professor.

'Ploof woo woo muffn plith a woogle,' said the hazy Mrs Flittersnoop, bustling up.

'Goo goo,' said the very young nothing-on-at-all Professor, trying to climb up the Colonel's trousers.

'How will my uniform come out?' said one of the photo sort of Colonels clanking out of the dining-room.

'What's this? What's this?' roared the real Colonel, catching sight of him. 'Impostor, scoundrel! That is not me at all, I'm me here,' he shouted and chased his photograph up the stairs. 'Impostor, scoundrel!' 'Will my uniform come out all right?' 'Wait till I catch you. Police, police!' 'Pass along p . . . Pass along p . . .' 'Goo goo,' 'Ploof woo woo muffn plith a woogle.'

It was more awful than ever. The real Professor dashed round a corner slap into the real Colonel, and each of them thought the other wasn't him at all, and while they were getting explained to each other three of the Mrs Flittersnoops changed hats, which probably made things no worse.

'Quick,' gasped the Professor after he had told the Colonel what had happened, so rapidly that the Colonel's head was nearly as fuzzy as the out-of-focus Mrs Flittersnoop. 'Must get blotting-paper, dry liquid off photos, then will go back into album.'

Round the house they dashed, brandishing blotters right and left. The little Professors were caught and blotted up quite easily, but Colonel Dedshott got away from himself three times, and the Mrs Flittersnoop in fancy dress kept dodging the Professor round the banisters.

Slap slap, bump, bang, scuffle biff. 'Don't take it yet, I've got the sun in my eyes. Hold it perfectly still . . .' 'How will my uniform come out?' 'Ploof woo woo muffn . . .' Round and round the house, up and down the stairs. The real Professor and Colonel caught each other eight times. The half policeman was hopping about like a canary shouting his half piece half at the top of his voice. Some of the Professors had got hold of blotting-paper and were joining in the chase. Then a window blew open and the draught from the open front door blew them all out of it and down the road, for they were beginning to get a bit light now that the effects of the liquid were wearing off.

'After them!' panted the Colonel, drawing his sword and falling over it.

Out they dashed and down the road. Clouds of Professors and Mrs Flittersnoops were all over the place. A real policeman stopped and gaped at the half policeman, who shouted 'Pass along p . . .' for the last time and then went *zzzzzzzp*, back into the photograph he had come from, with the Professor aged twenty.

'Hurray, hurray!' roared the Colonel, throwing his hat in the air and not bothering to catch it, when it landed on the real Professor's head. 'Victory! The enemy is routed!'

And so they were, for the sun had come out and quickly dried the wonderful liquid off the unreasonable crowd of extra sort of people and soon the road was strewn with photographs which the Colonel and the Professor carefully burned, making an awful smoke all over the place, but never mind.

Next day a note came up from Mrs Flittersnoop, written on the back of an elephant, to say that if the Professor would promise not to do it again she would come back.

'Well, well, well,' he said. 'All the liquid has been used up and I've forgotten the recipe so I shan't be able to do it again, thank goodness. But it was most instructive.'

So back came Mrs Flittersnoop, and the Professor wrote a book about his wonderful liquid but nobody believed it.

From *The Incredible Adventures of Professor Branestawm*

Branestawm's
Cross-Figure Puzzle

Each clue indicates a number. The result must add up to 30 across each horizontal, down each vertical and across each diagonal.

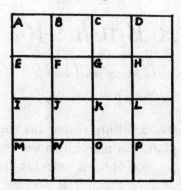

CLUES

A The race for Oxford and Cambridge.
B A trio.
C Said to be unlucky.
D Indians (Sikhs).
E A handful of fingers.
F A fortnight's-worth of days.
G A duck.
H For playing cricket.
I Twins.
J For skittling down.
K Deadly sins.
L Months.
M Rugby players.
N Corners of the world.
O Comes before a Jack.
P ... and only.

For solution see page 262

From *Professor Branestawm's Compendium*

A Brush with the Artists

A large square envelope rested on the Professor's breakfast plate. He put it into the toast rack and tried to open a piece of toast with his knife, but Mrs Flittersnoop came to the rescue and extracted from the envelope a large square card with wriggly gilt edges and very superior printing made to look as if it were writing.

'The Management of the Royal Pagwell Society of Arts requests the pleasure of the company of' and then, in rather squiggly writing, 'Professor Branestawm and friend' followed by 'at an exhibition of the work of Paul Palette-Brushleigh, Esq. R.P.S.A., to be opened by The Right Honourable Lord Pagwell of Pagwell at 3 p.m. on March 10.' Then it added in very small type, as if it hoped you wouldn't be able to read it, 'Tea will be served.'

'Ah, um, pictures,' said the Professor. 'Most

interesting, I have no doubt. What friend can I take? Colonel Dedshott, I fear, would not appreciate pictures unless they were battle pictures and Dr Mumpzanmeazle seems to, ah, fancy only pictures of people's veins and muscles. Had it been an exhibition of stained glass windows I could have taken the Vicar, and no doubt Monsieur Bonmonjay of the Pagwell Hotel would have been interested if the pictures were still life, showing collections of food. But I believe Mr Palette-Brushleigh specialises in rather extraordinary paintings. So I wonder who I could take. Yes, yes of course! Mrs Flittersnoop!' he called.

'Another egg, Professor?' asked Mrs Flittersnoop.

'Ah, ha ha, no,' said the Professor. 'My voice may have sounded a little cracked, but I was not laying an egg.'

'No, indeed, I'm sure, sir,' said Mrs Flittersnoop who began to see that this would be one of those days when the Professor was going to be jolly.

'You must, ah, come with me to this exhibition,' said the Professor, waving the card and making his tea go cold. 'You like pictures, I believe?' he added.

'Well yes, sir, thanking you kindly,' said Mrs Flittersnoop, who *was* very fond of the pictures when they had exciting-looking gentlemen in them and plenty to cry about. But these weren't going to be moving pictures and she wasn't too sure if she would enjoy herself. But, of course, she was much too polite to say so.

The Grand Gallery of the Royal Pagwell Society of Arts was crowded. There were pictures, and there were people who had come to see them. There were arty-looking persons with beards, who were the ones who hung the pictures and swept the floors and cleaned the windows, and there were some severe-looking people with short hair and rimless eyeglasses and a very bank manager look, who were artists. There were tastefully arranged tea-tables and there was Lord Pagwell, who although he wasn't a very large man, always seemed to give the impresion that the room was full of him, and on these occasions he was certainly very full of himself.

But before he could start opening the exhibition the Secretary of the Arts Society popped up and gave the audience what he called a brief history of the Society, which took a very long time. Then a big beard with someone behind it got up and said that Lord Pagwell needed no introduction, but took simply ages to introduce him. After that, Lord Pagwell, who had brought pages of notes for his speech, secretely tore them all up and said this was a time for pictures, not words, and he declared the exhibition open.

'Er, ah, hum,' said Professor Branestawm, looking at the pictures through various spectacles.

One picture was called 'Loneliness' and consisted of hundreds of coloured dots of different shapes. Another was 'Trees by a River' and showed two very upstanding lettuces and a cup of tea. There was one very narrow picture, five feet long and three inches high, painted purple all over with a black squiggle in one corner, and that was called 'Evening'.

'Er, ah, most interesting, but most puzzling and

exceedingly not understandable,' murmured the Professor, looking rather nervously at a big picture of ferocious eyes clustered round a frying pan.

'Well, I never did, sir,' said Mrs Flittersnoop, caught between a picture of two bent lampposts in a bath and one of rows and rows of empty bottles, all the wrong shape. 'They're not very good, are they? Indeed, I'm sure, sir, my little nephew could do better.'

'Pah!' snorted a voice behind them, and a very skinny, wild-looking little man with a lot of hair said, 'You betray ignorance, madam. Your small middle class mind fails to appreciate the deeper meaning behind these pictures.'

'Ah!' said Professor Branestawm, who wasn't going to have Mrs Flittersnoop spoken to like that. 'And who are you, pray, who can appreciate the inner meaning of this, er, um, ah, tarradiddle of paint splashing?'

'I am Paul Palette-Brushleigh,' said the skinny little man, drawing himself up to his full height, which was nothing to speak of. 'You look an intelligent man. How can you tolerate such un-informed criticism from your comapanion?'

'I am Professor Branestawm,' said the Professor, taking all his spectacles off and staring at the skinny little man, who looked rather like one of his own pictures. 'And I, ah, agree entirely with this lady's comments.'

'Huh!' snorted Mr Palette-Brushleigh, shaking his hair about and making quite a draught. 'And I suppose you, like your companion's relative, could do better yourself?'

'Yes,' snapped the Professor. 'I not only can produce better pictures, but I *shall*. I shall invent a machine, my good sir,' he said, 'that will paint better pictures than you have ever dreamed of! And what is more,' he flung out his arms and knocked Mrs Flittersnoop's hat crooked, 'they will be pictures that look like something!'

Mr Palette-Brushleigh snorted. 'Look like something indeed!' 'But the Professor didn't hear him. He and Mrs Flittersnoop had gone to tea, which was one of those buffet kind of teas, where you helped yourself to as much as you could eat or as much as you could carry, whichever was the greater, and then looked round and found there was nowhere to sit.

'I have arranged', said the Professor to Colonel Dedshott next day, after telling him about the exhibition, 'to invent a picture-painting machine and the Royal Pagwell Society of Arts has agreed to exhibit a selection of the pictures it will produce.'

'My word, jolly good!' said Colonel Dedshott, who reckoned that anyone who could paint a picture of anything that looked like something was mighty clever. 'That'll show 'em!'

'I am also . . .' went on the Professor, putting the Colonel's medals straight as some of them had jumped over the wrong side to the front when the Colonel got a bit excited. 'I am also going to, ah, demonstrate my machine to the Society,' he said.

'Bravo!' said the Colonel, making a note to have some Catapult Cavaliers lurking about at the demonstration in case there was trouble.

'And I thought perhaps,' added the Professor, 'that you would be good enough to sit for your portrait when my machine is ready.'

'Ha, yes, rather!' cried the Colonel, who was always good enough to have his picture done, whether it was by exotic artists or little black cameras. He had an enormous painting over his fireplace of an ancestor of his, Major Dedshott, painted against a background of fire, cannon-balls and clashing swords which was supposed to represent the Major at Waterloo. But as a matter of fact, although he had been at the Battle of Waterloo, it was a long time before he became a Major, and he was only there to help clean the Duke of Wellington's Wellington Boots, which he did well out of cannon-ball range, nowhere near any clashing swords and with no fire except the one in the grate.

Professor Branestawm's Picture-painting Machine was giving him more trouble than his inventions usually did when he was inventing them because, being an artistic machine, it was a bit temperamental. It insisted on trying to paint autumn trees on the Professor's shirt-front because it couldn't bear to see anything white without wanting to paint on it. It put several ruined castles on the inventory walls, which wasn't necessary as previous inventions had already made them look ruined enough. And twice it painted miniatures of railway stations on the buns Mrs Flittersnoop brought for the Professor's elevenses.

But at last the Professor got it finished and reasonably tamed, and set it to work. And very soon the Professor and his machine were out and about in the Pagwells, immortalising the landscape, the buildings and some of the people, in paint.

Then along went the pictures to the Royal Pagwell Society of Arts, in a van from the Pagwell Furnishing Company, supplied by the manager, Mr Chintsbitz, who had a huge beard and felt well disposed to artists. The Picture-painting Machine went separately, in Mrs Flittersnoop's cousin Bert's cart, covered up with plastic tarpaulins so as to be as secret as possible.

The great day of the Branestawm exhibition of mechanically painted pictures arrived, right on the correct day, and Lord Pagwell, who loved opening exhibitions, actually made a speech lasting several minutes, most of which was taken up by frightfully funny stories about nearly everything except pictures.

But at last the exhibition was prized open, and

cries of delight went up from everybody except a group of very contemporary artists, led by Mr Palette-Brushleigh, who shrank most energetically from anything in a frame if you could see which way up it was supposed to hang.

Professor Branestawm's machine had certainly excelled itself. There was a lovely landscape of Pagwell Canal by moonlight and one of the Pagwell gasworks in a thunderstorm. There were beautiful pictures of trees and forest glades and country cottages that would have graced the most expensive box of chocolates anyone could wish for. There were five portraits of Colonel Dedshott which would have terrified any enemy who happened to be within eyeshot. There was a still life of one of Mrs Flittersnoop's rice puddings that looked much less still and ten times as lively as any respectable pudding coud hope to be. There were pictures to delight the heart, to please the eye, to sooth the savage breast and exalt the downhearted.

The exhibition was an enormouse success. All the pictures were sold, the portraits of Colonel Dedshott to Colonel Dedshott, the landscapes to Farmer Plownough, who enjoyed looking at a field he didn't have to plough, and to people who always like a nice bit of English countryside as long as the weather was fine, which it always was in these pictures. The Mayor bought a picutre of Pagwell Town Hall painted almost life-size with him standing in the doorway apparently holding the whole thing up. The Vicar bought a rather sweet little one of Pagwell Church with a halo round it. Lord Pagwell, who owned the

Pagwell Publishing Company, bought the Flittersnoop rice pudding to use as the cover of a cookery book. And a threatening picture of very spidery machinery was acquired by Pagwell College. Mr Stinckz-Bernagh, the science master, thought it would be useful for demonstrating the impossibility of having five right angles in a square.

'And now, ladies and gentlemen,' said Lord Pagwell, after banging on an empty turnpentine tin the Society had supplied for the purpose, to get attention, 'we shall now see a demonstration of Professor Branestawm's wonderful machine actually painting pictures.'

'Here is the machine itself,' said Professor Branestawm, whisking a cloth dramatically off, and producing the machine, which looked at the assembled company as if it didn't think much of any of them as oil paintings.

'First of all we have the picture size adjuster,' said the Professor, moving corner-shaped bits of frame in and out, 'as it would be most inconvenient to set the machine painting a six-foot landscape if one had only a two-foot canvas. Here we have the subject-choosing dials.' The Professor pointed to a row of knobs labelled Landscape, Seascape, Interior, Still life and Portrait. 'This device,' he explained, 'makes it unnecessary to go out to nature in order to paint landscapes if you do not wish to do so.'

'Ha!' exclaimed the Advanced Artists, who never went out to nature as they were scared stiff of cows in fields.

The Professor adjusted his spectacles, turned the

machine round, and wheeled it forward a bit.

'Here we have the perspective corrector,' he explained.

'Boo!' cried the Advanced Artists, who didn't agree with perspective because it was too difficult to do.

'This is the colour harmony discipliniser,' said the Professor, pointing to an oval wheel, 'to obviate any possibility of getting discordant clashes of objectionable colour.'

'Yah!' shouted the Advanced Artists, whose main idea was to get as many clashes of colour as possible just to show that they weren't bound by the inhibiting rules of commonplace art.

'And here are the colour racks, the brush holders and the form analyser,' the Professor went on.

'Bravo, what!' grunted Colonel Dedshott, who didn't see why the Advanced Artists shoud be the only ones to make remarks.

'I shall now set the machine to paint a picture,' said the Professor, stuffing all his five pairs of spectacles into three pockets, turning knobs and pressing buttons on the machine. He put a large canvas into the picture holder and pulled a lever.

Ziz, poppety, slop, splosh, went the machine, landing a dab of Prussian Blue accurately in the middle of the forehead of the largest Advanced Artist who had advanced a bit too near for its liking.

After a few minutes the whizzing and popping stopped. The Professor and two picture-hanging assistants lifted the picture out of the machine and put it on an easel.

'Good gracious!' exclaimed Lord Pagwell.

'*Most* remarkable,' said the Vicar.

'Bravo!' cried Colonel Dedshott.

'Pah!' snorted the Advanced Artists.

The picture showed a landscape with trees of all kinds, three fields, one ploughed, one full of daisies and one full of assorted cows, a river with yachts, an old water mill, seven fancy cottages, two ruined castles, a pond with ducks, three bridges, a farm with horses and hens, two gardens full of flowers, a woodland glade, a seashore with liners in the distance, a church with two spires, and some distant mountains, all seen through a window with abstract curtains in front of which was a table with a bowl of fruit, some flowers in a copper jug and a portrait of Lord Pagwell.

It was the picture to end all pictures.

There was a tremendous buzzing of conversation and uttering of excitable exclamations as everyone crowded round the picture and Lord Pagwell had to hit the empty turpentine tin five times to get silence for his next announcement.

'For the benefit of those who were unable to come today,' he said, 'Professor Branestawm has kindly consented to do another demonstration here tomorrow at the same time.'

That night, when the moon turned the Gallery of the Royal Pagwell Society of Arts into a very picturesque mixture of deep purple shadows and pale green moonlight, a number of murky figures crept in.

They were members of the Way Ahead and Right Outside Group of Advanced Artists and they were bent on mischief. They were also bent nearly double so as not to be seen through the windows. They were going to muck up the Professor's beautiful painting machine because they didn't agree with being shown up and done down by a lot of cog-wheels.

'Hist!' they said, histing.

'Shush!' they said, shushing.

They histed and shushed their way round the machine, loosening screws and inserting plastic spanners of very bad design into the works. Then they crept out, still histing and shushing while the moon went on shining, never mind what Advanced Artists had been doing.

Next day the Professor arrived to find everybody there waiting to see the demonstration, some of whom hadn't seen it and just couldn't wait to see it now, and some who had seen it the day before and didn't believe it, and wanted to see it again and see if they didn't believe it again.

'I have been asked that the machine do a painting of Pagwell High Street,' said the Professor, taking the cover off.

He didn't notice anything wrong, because the Way Ahead and Right Outside Group of Advanced Artists had been very crafty in their machinations on the machine.

He put in a canvas, made adjustments and pulled a lever.

Squeeeeek, scraach! Bang! yelled the machine feeling something was wrong with it. *Splip, plop, splash,* red, green, pink and blue paint shot about. Several of the ladies received very unfashionable spotted dresses and one or two Advanced Artists looked as if they had technicolour measles.

The machine really got going. It painted not one picture but several. When the Professor did not feed canvases into it, it stretched out brush-holding arms and grabbed them. It painted pictures on top of Mr Palette-Brushleigh's pictures. It painted a portrait of the Mayor on the face of Mr Palette-Brushleigh. It did still lifes on rapidly running spectators.

'Help!' shouted the onlookers. 'Switch it off!'

The Professor pulled levers and twiddled dials, but he guessed it would make no difference and it didn't.

'Some miscreants have sabotaged the machine,' gasped the Professor, receiving a country cottage on the forehead.

'To the rescue!' shouted Colonel Dedshott, who had taken the precaution of bringing some Catapult Cavaliers again.

'Man the lifeboats!' roared Commander Hardaport (Retired), who had come to see seascapes.

Slap, plop, squirt, whizzy dizzy splosh! went the machine, busily doing abstract paintings on the windows.

'Stop it!' 'Help!' 'Fire!' 'Police!' yelled the crowd.

Colonel Dedshott and the Catapult Cavaliers descended on the machine and were painted shocking pink and lime green in hexagons before they could get a blow in.

'Smash it!' yelled the Advanced Artists, retreating before a fusillade of ruined castles and picturesque cottages.

'Action stations!' roared Commander Hardaport (Retired), receiving a rough sea with rocks in the waistcoat as he launched himself in line ahead at the machine.

At last the machine ran out of paint and quietened down.

'Now's our chance to bust it!' yelled the Advanced Artists advancing threateningly.

'No, you don't, by Jove!' cried Colonel Dedshott. The rainbow-coloured Catapult Cavaliers lined up to protect the machine.

'I take over this machine in the Queen's name!' cried Colonel Dedshott, saluting with a rose madder hand. 'Invaluable and invincible weapon against future enemies of the realm!' he declared.

Then the Catapult Cavaliers hoisted the machine on their shoulders and marched left, right, left, right, out of the Gallery followed by Colonel Dedshott and cries from the leftish and rightish artists.

Next day Professor Branestawm received a very military letter on buff paper from General Shatterfortz, thanking him for presenting his most formidable engine to the Army and assuring him that few enemies would have the courage to face its barrage of artistic ammunition, and adding that he was having it converted to hurl pictures of tanks and fortresses instead of churches and country cottages.

From *Professor Branestawm Up the Pole*

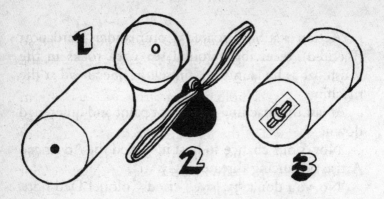

A Tin that Does
as You Tell It

Imagine having a small tin such as a cocoa tin or treacle tin, which you roll along the table. Then you say to it, 'Stop and come back to me!' and the tin stops and rolls back to you. You can also put the tin at the bottom of a slope and tell it to roll up, which it will do.

The Professor nearly wrecked the Pagwell gas-works, the railway station and the broadcasting station trying to get outrageous things to make this invention with. But at last he discovered he could do it with a tin, an elastic band, and a bit of lead.

Take an ordinary small round tin with a lid. In the bottom of the tin and in the lid, pierce a small hole with a sharp instrument such as a bradawl, as shown in Figure 1.

Now you want a strong elastic band a little shorter than the height of the tin. Pass the elastic band through the metal loop on a round fishing weight and tie it so that the weight is hanging in the centre of the elastic band, as in Figure 2. Now pass one end of the elastic band through the hole in the bottom of the tin, from inside. The easiest way to do this is to thread a piece of thin wire through the elastic band, twist the ends of the wire togther and then you can thread the wire through the hole easily. Pull the wire through until it brings the end of the elastic band through. Remove the wire and push a piece of matchstick through the elastic band to stop it from going back through the hole. Stick a piece of sticky tape over the matchstick to hold everything secure. See figure 3.

Now thread the opposite end of the elastic band through the lid of the tin, also from the inside, and fasten it with a matchstick and tape as before. Put the lid on the tin and you're ready.

You must choose a tin wide enough so that when the lid is on the tin and the tin is laid on its side, the weight doesn't quite touch the side of the tin.

If you roll the tin away from you, the lead weight will prevent the elastic band from going round with the tin. The elastic band will twist up and, after the tin has rolled a little way, the tension on the twisted elastic will make it stop. Then as the elastic untwists itself, it will cause the tin to roll back to you.

To make the tin roll uphill, hold it in your hands and turn it round, over and over, several times, or, if you like, roll it along the table some distance but don't let it roll back. You will now have the elastic inside the tin twisted up quite tightly and if you put the tin at the bottom of a gentle slop – nothing too steep – it will roll up the slope. But you must of course put it down the right way, so that if you have wound up the elastic by rolling the tin away from you along the table, you must turn the tin round to make it climb the slope.

In addition, if you stand the tin up while the elastic is still wound, the tin will give a spooky little shuffle and wobble. The more the elastic is would up, the more wobble it will do.

One day Professor Branestawm is going to invent an elastic motor car on this principle. It won't need any petrol. You just push it where you want to go, and then it will bring you back.

From *Professor Branestawm's Do-It-Yourself Handbook*

Branestawm's Cross-Figure Puzzle Solution

A 8	B 3	C 13	D 6
E 5	F 14	G 0	H 11
I 2	J 9	K 7	L 12
M 15	N 4	O 10	P 1

If you want to go really Branestawmy dotty, try making a Branestawmy Cross-Figure in decimals and see if you can work one out that adds up to point something or other. But mind your brains don't get oxidised.

The Monstrous Memorial

In front of Great Pagwell Station, in the middle of the station courtyard, stood a monument. A terrific monument. A highly ornamental and determined-looking pile. A very terror.

It had been there ever since the first Lord Pagwell (the present Lord Pagwell's father) was made a Lord. It had been built, or rather created, erected, put up and devised to commemorate the occasion. It had been designed with savage artistry by the celebrated sculptor, Herr von Phluffenhaar, and constructed with a special kind of ersatz stone invented by Professor Branestawm. The Professor had also invented into it one or two other things which no monument had ever possessed before.

It showed the first Lord Pagwell seated on a sort of throne shaped like the Loch Ness Monster, and surrounded by a set of green and purple mermaids because the first Lord Pagwell had been keen on the sea. Over his head was a fancy canopy to keep the rain off. This was trimmed by festoons of concrete lace and supported by knotted columns, and on top of it all was a kind of super-large sized ice-cream strucure with gilded pineapples.

The first Lady Pagwell didn't think much of it, but she said, if they were going to have it, then there should be a clock on it so that it would be of some use. So a clock there jolly well was. A very Branestawm of a clock that chimed the hours and quarters, told you the date, showed the phases of the moon, marked the temperature and indicated what the weather would be, though it always got it wrong. And at certain times of the day it gave a display of coloured lights and played the favourite tune of the first Lord Pagwell.

'I think it's time we got rid of it,' said the Mayor, at a Council meeting one day. 'It has outlived its usefulness.'

'Pah!' snorted the Drains Councillor, who didn't like the monument because it didn't need any drains. 'Monuments don't live and it never had any usefulness.'

'Oh yes, it did and still does,' protested the Town Clerk. 'It's a very useful place to meet people because everyone knows where it is.'

'It is a traffic hazard,' complained the Head Policeman, who had come to make sure nothing illegal was discussed. 'People run into it at night. If it was knocked down we could park cars there.'

The railway company was all in favour of having the monument done away with. People used to try to buy tickets at it, thinking it was a special cheap-rate tourist office. Others thought it was a waiting-room and wrote rude letters of complaint when they found it wasn't. And visitors to Great Pagwell were known to go inside it thinking it was a hotel and not be able to find the way out again, which meant rescuing them with the Fire Brigade. And it kept the sun out of the Station-master's sitting-room.

Lord Pagwell said he would be rather glad to see it go. He thought green and purple mermaids weren't quite in keeping with the dignity of his position and anyway it wasn't his memorial, it was his father's, and besides, Lady Pagwell had scraped a few rather expensive bits off her car on it because she always said she was sure the thing ran into her and not the other way round.

'Well, I, um, ah,' said Professor Branestawm. 'If everyone else wants the memorial removed I shall not stand in the way.' He felt standing in the way of memorial-removers might get him removed somewhere awkward too. 'It is, er, one of my very early pieces of work,' he said, 'done when I was very young and inexperienced, so it is hardly a memorial to my inventiveness.'

So the Great Pagwell memorial was to go. The station yard immediately became full of trucks and bulldozers and men with pickaxes and noisy drills. Would-be passengers couldn't get into the station and had to go round to the other side and come back across the footbridge.

Bang! Boom! Crash! The demolition started with great enthusiasm. Day and night the demolishers worked. But at the end of the two noisy weeks the memorial looked the same as ever, except that it had a bit more dust on it than usual.

'We can't shift un,' said the Head Demolisher. 'She been and bent all our drills, like, and the lads is getting fed up. One of 'em says as 'ow one o' them mermaids looks like his mother-in-law and he's afraid to touch it in case it hits back.'

'We had better call in the Army,' said the Mayor. 'After all, we've got all those soldiers doing nothing but march up and down. I reckon attacking the memorial would be good practice for them.'

General Shatterfortz was all for it. It meant he could issue orders. He could send round urgent memos. And he did.

The noise of road drills and bulldozers and pickaxes was replaced with the rumble of military wheels and the shouting of military commands. Colonel Dedshott was everywhere at once. The Army set about the job in style. First, regiments of military cleaners arrived with buckets and mops and thoroughly cleaned the memorial till it shone like a highly-polished jelly in bright sunshine. Then military painters arrived and touched up the paint. They re-gilded the gold pineapples, they made the whole thing as good as new.

'Can't have the Army operating against anything shabby,' grunted the General. 'Must get it all neat and polished up before we destroy it.'

At last the memorial was sufficiently spick and span to be knocked down. The artillery drew up with their best guns. The streets of Pagwell were cleared. The shops were shut, the children sent to stay with their aunts.

A very small, bristly Artillery Major drew himself up to his full height, which put rather a strain on his braces, and shouted in a voice that broke three of the railway station windows.

'Numbah one gun fiyah!'

Boom! Number one gun fired. When the smoke had cleared away the memoral was still there, but parts of it were a bit dirty and had to be washed again.

'Numbah two gun fiyah!' yelled the Major.

Boom!

The Major's voice chipped a bit of concrete lace off the canopy, but the shell bounced off the statue's waistcoat and blew a hole in the road.

All that day the Artillery Major screamed, 'Numbah something gun fiyah!' The guns boomed and banged. Clouds of smoke went up and came down again but the memorial only took on a slightly more sinsister sneer.

'All guns fiyah!' screeched the Major.

Boom! Bang! Bonketty boom!

One of the shells missed the memorial entirely and shot a little turret off the station, which dropped on the top of the memorial and made it even bigger than before.

But still not a single chip fell off the memorial.

'Fetch Professor Branestawm!' cried the Mayor, tearing his hair and wishing the memorial could be torn apart as easily. 'He invented the thing. Let him demolish it.'

'Er, um, ah,' said the Professor when he arrived. 'You must remember,' he said, 'that I invented a special material for this memorial, one that would withstand the rigours of the weather, need no maintenance and never decay.'

'Do you mean the thing is there for ever?' gasped the Mayor.

'When I was asked to devise this memorial,' said the Professor, 'I understood that it was to be in lasting memory of the first Lord, um, ah, Pagwell. If I had been told it was to be a temporary memorial, a

momentary monument, so to speak, I should have acted differently. However, since you wish this memorial demolished I will see what I can do.'

He went into his inventory to invent a memorial-demolishing machine. The first machine nearly demolished the inventory, the second one demolished the Professor's dinner and the third one demolished itself.

'Er, um,' said the Professor, putting custard into his coffee in mistake for milk and thinking it tasted rather better. 'Possibly a new kind of explosive with devastating but limited effect.'

To begin with that wasn't any good because nobody could make a hole in the monument to put the explosive in.

Then the Professor inserted some of the explosive into a gap between the mermaids and Lord Pagwell's throne. Everyone retired immediately, as if it were firework night, and the Professor set off the charge.

Bam, krarrsh! The explosive went off in a cloud of striped smoke. All the birds in Great Pagwell rose straight up in the air and then came down again. One of the mermaids now had an orange beard with blue spots but otherwise the memorial was unchanged.

Deadlock had been reached. There was Great Pagwell stuck with an immovable object in the shape of the Lord Pagwell Memorial, but where was the irresistible force to try to move it with?

That night there was the thunderstorm of the century.

'Ha!' said everyone, which sounded very strange if you happened to be listening. 'Now the memorial will be struck by lightning.'

And it was. The lightning struck it three times, then gave up and went away to strike something easier. The memorial remained unchanged, but a mermaid's head was slightly scorched.

Then two days later, without any warning, the indestructible memorial collapsed in a heap of coloured rubble.

'I can't understand it,' said the Professor, shaking his head. 'I can only conclude that the cumulative effect of pneumatic drills, high explosives, artillery fire, pickaxes and lightning must have set up some kind of secondary reaction within the molecules of the material, thus casuing delayed disintegration.'

Pagwell Council hadn't the least idea what he was talking about. But if they didn't understand why the memorial had demolished itself, they weren't going to argue, in case it reconsitituted itself when they weren't looking. In no time at all men in funny hats carried the memorial away in wheelbarrows, swept the place clean and left the station yard clear for cars to park illegally.

'Now,' said the Mayor, at the next Council meeting, 'what shall we have in place of the memorial? We can't leave the space empty, it looks so vacant.'

'Arrh,' said one of the Councillors, who always looked a bit vacant himself. 'How about a nice fountain?'

'We've already got a fountain,' said the Town Clerk, 'as you can see if you look out of the window.'

Another Councillor said it would be a good idea to have a hospital as the new memorial since that would be more useful. But there were already a great many hospitals in the Pagwells and not enough nurses to go round.

'I suggest a clock tower,' said the Town Clerk, who always forgot to wind up his watch and depended on public clocks to run his private life.

'Yes, that might encourage the trains to run to time,' said a Councillor, who managed to catch a train only by arriving at the station just too late to catch the previous one.

'But the old memorial had a clock on it,' protested another Councillor. 'We don't want all that trouble over again.'

'Nonsense,' cried the Mayor. 'It wasn't the clock that caused the trouble, it was the rest of it. Anyway we needn't have an elaborate clock that plays tunes and all that stuff. Just a nice, quiet, chiming clock.'

So Professor Branestawm was asked to invent a clock tower with a nice, quiet, chiming clock on it to go where the awful memorial used to be.

'No mermaids, mind,' said the Mayor. 'No fancy work, no outlandish ideas. And for goodness sake, make sure it doesn't obstruct the traffic. We don't want cars running into it as they did to the memorial.'

'Um, ah, er, yes,' said the Professor, mentally crossing out all the outlandish ideas he was having.

He went into his inventory and started inventing like mad. 'They shall have their nice, quiet clock tower,' he muttered. 'I won't give them any outlandish ideas. They're going to have the plainest, most ordinary, dull, unimaginative, miserable clock tower that ever was.'

They certainly did. The clock tower was dark black all over and chimed in a whisper. It stood on legs so that people could drive cars under it. It had no mermaids, no floral weaths, not even a fancy scroll.

But there's no pleasing some people, as they say. Letters began to pour in from the residents of Great Pagwell, complaining that the new clock tower was too quiet, too plain, too uninteresting and too nearly everything they thought it ought not to be.

Some people wanted the clock to show metric time because of the Common Market. Others *didn't* want it to be metric in case it meant they had only ten hours in a day instead of twelve. Some people said couldn't the clock tower be arranged to sell soft drinks and hard ice-creams for people waiting for trains. Others wanted it to have illuminated maps of Great Pagwell on it so that people could find their way about. Still others thought it would be nice to have a dovecote on top so that pigeons could fly in and out and make it look like a cuckoo clock tower.

One or two people wanted it to show news films. Mr Pryce-Rize would have liked it to broadcast news of the latest bargains at his supermarket. The Vicar was all for having the times of services posted on it and thought he might even conduct special clock tower services in it. Colonel Dedshott felt it would be a good saluting base for military parades and the Head Policeman said it ought to broadcast traffic instructions and dire warnings against parking cars anywhere at any any time.

'Pah!' snorted Professor Branestawm. He threw all the letters up in the air. 'Serves them right for having my other memorial destroyed. If they don't like it they can lump it.'

But lumping clock towers, especially Professor Branestawm clock towers, takes a bit of doing. Complaining is easier.

The situation was awful. But then, on the fifth morning after the clock tower was finished, it fell down half-way through striking eight and everyone near enough to hear it thought it was only four o'clock and went to sleep again. They would have been late for work but fortunately it was Sunday.

'You, um, ah, see what comes of trying to tell me what sort of clock tower to invent,' said the Professor to the Town Clerk, while the collapsed tower was being carted away. 'Now perhaps you will kindly let me, ah, um, know best.'

The next clock tower was the sort of thing you dream about when you've had too much supper. It had an illuminated clock that chimed and struck as often as possible and played tunes in between. It had ornamental balconies and fancy spires and exotic minarets. It gave out weather forecasts, it explained how to get to almost anywhere, it gave warning of the approach of trains and it sold you chocolate, lemonade-flavoured crisps and coconut-flavoured peanuts, if you put the right coins in the right slots and moved out of the way quickly enough to avoid getting the goods in your eye.

It was certainly the clock tower of all clock towers.

'I think I may, um, ah, say without fear, of, ah, contradiction,' said the Professor, 'that this time the Council will have nothing to complain of.'

But the new clock tower kept the sun out of the Station-master's sitting-room just as effectively as the old memorial had done. People still ran into it in their cars. Others tried to buy special cheap-rate tickets at it. Passengers still thought it was a waiting-room and wrote rude letters of complaint when they found it wasn't, and Lady Pagwell contined to scrape expensive bits off her car on it.

But it didn't have any mauve mermaids which was something.

From *Professor Branestawm Round the Bend*

How to Turn a Pack of Cards into Several Boxes

E asy enough, isn't it? You just take the pack and turn the cards into boxes by tipping them in. Ha, yes, but that's not what Professor Branestawm means. He means you actually *convert* the cards into boxes. This is how.

Take four cards, lay them in a row face down, and tape them together, allowing a little space between the cards, as in Figure 1.

Now take two more cards and cut a piece off each so as to make them square. The easiest way to do this is to lay a card down with another card across it, as in Figure 2. Draw lines where the two cards cross and cut along the lines. The two square pieces will form the ends of the box. Tape the cut ends of the square pieces to the two short sides of the last card of the row. See Figure 3. Then cut two small slots in the second card from the opposite end, as in Figure 3.

The slots must be large enough to push a piece of narrow ribbon through.

Next bring the outer cards together and tape them so that you have a sort of tube of cards. All the tape should be on the inside of the tube.

Attach the end of a piece of narrow ribbon, about 30 cm long, to one of the square cards. The best way to do this is to cut a slot at the free end of the card, pass the ribbon through and stick it down on the outside face of the card with sticky tape.

Now push the other end of the ribbon through one of the slots in the tube of cards, passing the ribbon up from inside the tube, and then down through the second slot. Fasten it to the top of the other half-card.

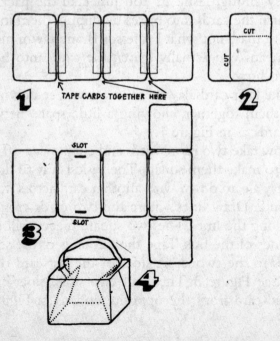

Fold the two square cards inwards and then, if you have allowed a little space between the cards when taping them, you will be able to fold the whole lot flat. Fold the folded cards over again, so making a little packet the size of one card.

There should be a loop of tape left above the slotted card. Take hold of this loop and give it a shake, and the packet will form itself into a little box. Figure 4 gives you a transparent view of the box, showing how the tape handle pulls the ends up into position to form a box.

You can make six of these boxes and if you put them all together in folded condition, with a single card face down on top, they will look very much like a pack of cards. You can do a sort of magic trick with them by saying they are a pack of cards, putting them into a hat and taking them out as boxes.

From *Professor Branestawm's Do-It-Yourself Handbook*

The Branestawm
Church Service

Professor Branestawm was immersed in Christmas card sending. And he was doing it most methodically.

'I, um, ah, must take care not to get things muddled up,' he said to Mrs Flittersnoop. 'It wouldn't do at all for our friends to get the wrong cards or not get them at all.'

'Yes indeed, I'm sure, sir,' said Mrs Flittersnoop, who'd had an exceedingly rowdy card from the Professor last Christmas because he'd picked up two at once in the shop by mistake, and had put the wrong one back without noticing.

'To make sure I don't forget to post them,' he said, 'I am going to address one to myself. Then when that arrives it will do two things, it will show that I have posted the others and it will remind me not to post another lot.'

Mrs Flittersnoop had nothing to say to that, as

she'd had to go and answer the door. Not that the door was in the habit of asking questions, but the bell had just rung, which meant someone had called.

It turned out to be the Vicar with smiles and good wishes and a calendar with a picture of Great Pagwell Church.

'Ah, good morning, Professor,' said the Vicar, 'I wonder if I might take advantage of your most ingenious mind to help me solve a rather awkward problem connected with the church.'

'Ah, yes,' said the Professor. He sometimes had awkward problems connected with the church himself, because when he went there with Mrs Flittersnoop he always got so interested in working out complicated mathematical sums with the numbers on the hymn board that he found himself a bit out of step with the service. If he knelt down, he found everyone else standing up, and when he stood up, everyone else sat down. Then when the plate came round he was apt to say, 'Oh, ah, thank you,' and take a coin and try to eat it, thinking he was at a party and snacks were being handed round. But he was only too pleased for people to take advantage of his most ingenious mind, though it was by no means certain that it would solve problems, awkward or otherwise. In fact, it was much more likely to create them. But this didn't seem to deter the Vicar, who was professionally good at having faith in people and he had great faith in the Professor, though goodness knows why.

Mrs Flittersnoop found some suitable organ music on the radio, while the Vicar explained his problem to the Professor.

'People are not coming to church enough,' he said. 'That is to say not enough of them are coming to church, if you follow me.'

'Ah,' said the Professor, 'but if people follow you they will undoubtedly come to church, will they not?'

The radio changed over from a deeply religious oratorio to a programme of Hot Spot Pop Tops.

'Ah, yes, indeed,' said the Vicar. 'But the fact remains Great Pagwell Church is half empty for the services.'

'Well,' said the Professor, 'that means it is half full, which isn't bad.'

'Ah, but not good enough, I fear,' said the Vicar, while Mrs Flittersnoop smothered the Flaming Friends pop group on the radio and brought in cups of coffee and little cakes arranged in a cross on the plate to make them look suitable for the Vicar.

'We want the church filled,' went on the Vicar, 'but the trouble is my parish is so extensive, people have rather a long way to go so they tend to stop at home and listen to services on the radio, which I am afraid does very little good to our collections for the building fund to enlarge the church.'

'But why enlarge the church if you don't, um, ah, get enough people to fill it?' asked the Professor.

'One must move with the times,' answered the Vicar, 'and hope that in due course more people will be attracted to the church. Then it would be a great pity, nay almost a disaster, if the church were not big enough to accommodate them.'

'Um, ah, now, Vicar,' said Professor Branestawm,

arranging his five pairs of spectacles in their best thinking order, 'you say it is too far for people to go to your church. Then why not take your church to the people?'

'Dear me,' laughed the Vicar. 'I fear it is rather too immovable for that.'

'A travelling church!' said the Professor, waving his hands and making the Vicar's coffee go cold. 'Something to go round and round-up the non-church-goers,' he went on. 'You must do a little recruiting, Vicar. Go out and persuade them that your church is worth a little trouble to visit. I will look into the matter and see what I can invent.'

'That is most kind of you,' said the Vicar and he went out saying two small prayers, one of thanks for being able to get the Professor to help and another of hope that the Professor's help wouldn't turn out more disastrous than usual.

Professor Branestawm saw him out, and then went out himself to post his Christmas cards.

'Dear me, here's one addressed to me,' he said, finding the one he'd addressed to himself. 'How silly of me.' So he left it behind and posted the others.

When he got back home, he went into his inventory to invent a travelling church in which the Vicar could tour his parish to round-up radio-listening parishioners and get them to come to his live three-dimensional church in the round, so to speak.

One week and several inventions later the Professor came down to breakfast and asked:

'Is there a Christmas card for me from myself?'

Mrs Flittersnoop said there wasn't.

'Ah,' said the Professor and the complicated explanations began. 'That means I forgot to post the Christmas cards to the other people we want to send them to. You see, I sent one to myself, so that if it arrived I'd know I'd posted the others, but if it didn't that would mean I had forgotten to post the rest. Well it hasn't come, so I didn't post them and we must send them now.'

So he and Mrs Flittersnoop addressed another lot of cards and Mrs Flittersnoop posted them herself this time to make sure. But since the Professor had already posted the other cards, though not the one to himself, everyone got two cards from him. But they reckoned that was the sort of thing the Professor might do, so everything was all right after all, and the Professor went back to inventing his travelling church, while the Vicar went on preaching long sermons to very short congregations.

At last the Branestawm travelling Church was finished. It looked rather like a caravan with stained glass windows and a steeple. It had a pulpit for preaching recruiting sermons from. It had an organ that played rousing hymns, a peal of bells to bring the people along to hear the sermons, and over the pulpit an angel with a trumpet instead of a horn.

'Bless me!' exclaimed the Vicar when he saw it. 'I, er, really do not know what the Bishop will say about this.'

But the Bishop, who had an urgent date to

confirm a clump of schoolchildren before they grew up too much, didn't say anything, though he did wonder rather a lot.

'I will accompany you on your first round,' said the Professor. 'Show you how everything works.'

They got in. The Professor pressed a button and the organ started playing the can-can. The Professor hurriedly switched over to 'O come, All Ye Faithful' and drove off, just mising a number 38½ bus, which he didn't want to catch anyway.

The mobile church went humming and hymning along Church Street, down Temple Lane, past several cross roads, through Noel Street, Parish Lane, Bell Avenue, and Spire Lane, until the Vicar called, 'Stop here! This is a good rural spot.'

It was Pagwell Halfpenny, certainly rural but not very hopeful-sounding for collections.

'Now, let us see if we get a congregation,' said the Vicar. 'I think we might give a peal or two on the bells to attract the populace.'

The Professor pulled levers and the bells rang out *ding dong, dong ding, dong dong*, as bells like doing.

'Ah, here they come,' said the Vicar.

The first lot was a group of little boys who thought the Travelling Church was an ice cream van, but the Vicar couldn't even offer them a sundae, which seems strange. Then a pretty girl asked the Professor if he would marry her. But she had mistaken him for the Vicar, and what she really meant was that she wanted him to marry her to someone else. Several very country ladies thought the Travelling Church was a travelling supermarket and arrived with baskets, hoping to get groceries at something off, but only got the Vicar's recruiting sermon which went on and on.

Another lady brought her baby along to be christened, but, alas, there was no font in the caravan, not even a kitchen sink, as the Professor hadn't thought it would be needed. Someone suggested holding the baby's head under the village drinking fountain, but the Vicar hurriedly began another sermon.

They did rather better at the their next stop, which was Pagwell Hassett, and better still at Pagwell-under-Water, and, by the time they got to Pagwell-in-the-Maze, people were queuing up to hear the Vicar.

'Well, I think our mission has been very successful,' beamed the Vicar when they got back.

Next Sunday his church had even fewer people than usual.

'I really don't undersand it,' he said.

Soon the Travelling Church was doing a roaring service. People were queuing to attend it, and the Vicar added to his sermon a few choice hymns.

'But this is really ridiculours!' he creid. 'People are going to the Travelling Church, but they aren't coming here to the main church.'

'I, um, ah, rather think your mission has been too successful, Vicar,' said the Professor. 'It is so much easier for them to attend your Travelling Church than to travel into Great Pagwell to the main church.'

'Ah,' said the Vicar, 'then perhaps having attracted them to the Travelling Church, we should then bring them here for the service instead of having it in the Travelling Church.'

But that didn't work because the Travelling Church couldn't cope with the rush of people. At each place it visited it was soon filled with people attending the service, but they then got out and the church went on and filled up at the next stop. But when the Vicar started bringing the people to his main church he could, of course, bring only one Travelling Churchful at a time and, by the time he went back and collected another congregation from the next place, the first lot had grown tired of waiting and had gone home.

'We must have a fleet of Travelling Churches!' cried Professor Branestawm.

'Good gracious!' gasped the Vicar. He didn't know whether to be elated, or appalled, or astonished, or doubtful, or mystified at the idea of a fleet of Travelling Churches.

'I don't know what the Bishop will say,' he said.

But the Bishop was too busy arguing with the Dean about the Cathedral roof to say anything.

After several weeks of church-building noises in the Professor's inventory, with Mrs Flittersnoop not knowing what things were coming to, she was sure, but hoped it was all for the best, the fleet of Travelling Churches was ready.

'But I can't drive them all myself,' said the Vicar. 'We must call for volunteers.'

That was easy. Colonel Dedshott instantly offered to drive one, and Commander Hardaport (Retired) reckoned he could navigate a church. Miss Frenzie shot off enthusiastically in one with all bells changing, and the Mayor found driving a nice quiet restful church rather easier than laying foundation stones and opening bazaars.

So the follwing Sunday the Vicar had his church full and three-quarters, with people standing and even some lined up outside listening through the windows.

But after a bit the Travelling Churches became redundant because people thought while they were queuing up waiting for them to arrive they might as well queue up for their local bus, which ran rather more frequently, and which stopped right outside Great Pagwell Church.

But the Vicar was delighted. He had a nice full church to preach to, nice fat collections came in, and everybody was happy.

So he gave the Travelling Churches to Pagwell Council, who used them to give old-age pensioners holidays in the country. And the pensioners found the countryside always looked nice and bright and colourful through the stained glass windows whether the sun was shining or not.

From *Professor Branestawm's Perilous Pudding*

A Tower of
Match-boxes

You can build a tower of match-boxes, standing them one on top of another until you have perhaps eight or nine of them, and you can pick up the tower and move it without the match-boxes collapsing.

Just try it with some match-boxes and you'll find they'll fall over as soon as you move them. But not if you use the Professor Branestawm's highly special and deadly secret method of non-collapsing construction.

First you want a base to stand the match-box tower on. This must have an oblong hole in it just large enough to take the end of a match-box drawer. You can make this out of a piece of wood about 10 cm square in which you cut a hole of the right size. But an easier way to make the stand is to find a small box, such as empty chocolate box (emptying chocolate boxes is a lovely job – you just eat the chocolates) or any small carboard box. Stand the drawer of a match-box on its end in the middle of the lid of the box, draw round it, and cut the piece out with a Stanley 99 knife. The hole should be a close but not too tight fit for the drawer of the match-box.

Build your match-box tower by standing the first match-box on end over the hole and pushing the drawer down into the hole. This anchors it to the box. Figure 1. Now take your second box and as you stand it on the first, push the drawer down into the space left by the drawer in the first box. Continue like this with all the boxes and finally lay a match-box across the top of the tower to hide the fact that the drawers are pushed down. Figure 2.

You can now pick up the tower, holding it by the base, and move it about. The boxes won't collapse because they're all anchored to one another.

From *Professor Branestawm's Do-It-Yourself Handbook*

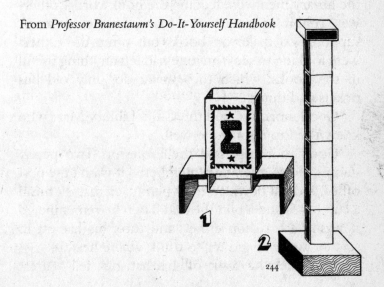

244

The Professor
Borrows a Book

Things were busy in the library at Great Pagwell when Professor Branestawm walked in. Some of the library men were feeding the bookworms, others were rubbing out the pencil marks that people aren't supposed to make on books but often do. Others were looking to see if anyone had left anything useful in the books, which they never do, only old bus tickets and things.

'Good morning,' said the Chief Library Man, who knew the Professor quite well.

'Good morning,' said the Professor. 'Two penny stamps, please,' then he remembered it wasn't the post office, and put down an extra penny, 'er, that is I mean a cup of tea and a bun,' he said. Then he remembered it wasn't a tea-shop either, and took his hat off to scratch his head and try to think where he was.

And when he took off his hat, out fell a great

crowd of papers. They shot all over the floor. They fluttered under tables and out of windows.

'Allow me,' said the Library Man, and, jumping over the counter quite easily because he was very sporting and could jump gates, he helped the Professor to pick up the papers. The Professor picked up two and dropped one of them again, while the Chief Library Man picked up the rest.

'Now, let me see,' said the Professor, turning over the papers and dropping some again, 'what did I want? It was a book about something.' He dropped some more papers, looked at the others through his near-sighted glasses, and then remembered he had written what he was looking for on the back of his collar, the night before. So he had to get the Library Man to read it out for him.

'*The Life and Likings of a Lobster,*' he read out.

'Yes,' said the Professor, fastening up the safety pins which he had on his coat instead of the buttons that had all come off. 'One of those, please, not too new.'

The Chief Library Man called a not-so-chief Library Man, who called a quite ordinary, unimportant sort of Library Man. And he went off and climbed ladders and got himself all dusty, poking about on shelves. And at last, when they thought he must have found an interesting adventure book and stopped to read it, back he came.

'*The Life and Likings of . . .*' he began, but the Professor grabbed the book out of his hand, opened it, and rushed out, reading it, putting his foot in the pail of soapy water the charwoman was cleaning the steps with, and getting half-way home with the pail stuck on his foot before it fell off.

The next morning the Professor could not find the book anywhere. He looked through his near-sighted glasses and his long-sighted glasses, and all his other glasses. He even looked through the glasses he used to look for the other pairs of glasses with when he lost them. But still he couldn't find it.

'Mrs Flittersnoop,' he called, 'have you seen a book with one of those green library covers? It's about lobsters. I had it last night, and now it's gone.'

'No, sir, that I haven't,' she said, 'and not that I'd touch it if I had, being most particular to leave things alone since . . .'

'Of course,' said the Professor hurriedly, so that Mrs Flittersnoop shouldn't go on and tell him about her cousin's husband's little girl, who was either just going to have measles, or had just had them.

Then he put on his hat and went across to the library at Little Pagwell. 'Have you got a book called *The Life and Likings of a Lobster*?' he asked the Chief Library Man.

'Certainly,' said the man, and he actually went and fetched it himself.

'Ta,' said the Professor, and went out leaving it on the counter, and had to come back for it.

After a fortnight had gone by it was time to take back to the library at Great Pagwell the book he had borrowed from there. But he had lost it, so he couldn't take it back.

'I'll have to take this one back,' said the Professor. So back he took it, and that was all right, because he was able to take it out again the next day and return it to the Library at Little Pagwell, so he didn't have any fines to pay at either place for keeping it too long.

Then he took the book out of the Little Pagwell library again the next day, and went home to read it a bit more.

'As long as I keep taking it back to Great Pagwell when the time's up,' he said, 'and getting it back next day and taking it over to Little Pagwell, it will be all right, and nobody will know I've lost the other book.'

You see both books had green library covers, so they both looked alike.

Then, what must the Professor go and do but lose the other book, the one that belonged to Little Pagwell.

'Dear, dear; that *is* a nuisance,' he said, and he

hunted for it like anything. He looked under the sofa, but all he found there was a bone Mrs Flittersnoop's sister's dog had left there weeks ago. He looked in the coal cellar and under the sink and at the back of the gas stove. He looked in all the places where a book isn't likely to be as well as all the places where it might be. And still he couldn't find it.

'Well,' he said, pushing all his five pairs of spectacles up a bit higher, 'I'll have to go to still another library and get another copy of the book.'

So he went and got one from the library at Upper Pagwell, took it to the library at Great Pagwell where it was just due, and handed it in. Next day he took it out again, and gave it in at the Little Pagwell Library. And so by taking it round in turn to all three libraries he still manage to stop any of them from knowing he had lost the books.

Then, bothered if he didn't lose *that* book, too!

'This is awful,' groaned the Professor. 'Whatever can be happening to all these books? It can't be the mice because we haven't any, and Mrs Flittersnoop does not read anything but story books with paper covers. She doesn't even read cookery books. I wish she did.'

He took off all his five pairs of spectacles, cleaned them and put them on again, getting them all mixed up and wondering why his smoked sun-glasses didn't magnify things.

Well, or course, in the end he just had to go off to the library at Lower Pagwell and get another copy of *The Life and Likings of a Lobster* there. And he had to keep going round with that one book to all four libraries, giving it in one day and taking it out the next.

Then he lost that book, too. Yes, he did, the careless man. And he kept on getting more and more copies of the book from more and more libraries, and losing them one after the other.

He had a book out of the library at Pagwell Town and Pagwell Village. He had one from Old Pagwell and New Pagwell, from North Pagwell and from South Pagwell, and another from West Pagwell, as well as Pagwell Central. He had one from Pagwell Hill and Pagwell Docks, not to mention Pagwell Gardens.

Yes, he took copies of the same book out of all these different libraries, and kept losing them until at last he had fourteen libraries to keep going, on only one book.

Now each library let him keep their book for fourteen days, so the Professor was just able to avoid paying a fine for keeping it too long. But every day he had to rush round to the library that had the book, take it out, dash off to the library where it was due next, and give it in again. It was terrible. He had no time to read the book. He had hardly time for meals. He got thinner and thinner through having to dash about so much. And he simply dared not stop rushing from library to library, because if he once let the book be a day late at one library, the fines would start getting bigger and bigger.

'Oh, what shall I do – what shall I do?' he cried, trying to tear his hair, only there wasn't enough of it.

Then he went to see his friend, Colonel Dedshott,

of the Catapult Cavaliers, to see if he could help.

'Lobsters!' said the Colonel when the Professor told him the title of the book. 'I like 'em, but they give me dreams.'

'Never mind that,' said the Professor. 'Tell me what I can do about the books I've lost. This rushing about is too much for a man of my age, whatever my age is. I can never remember.'

'Sorry, Professor,' said the Colonel, 'but I'm not going to get mixed up in any more of your adventures. All I can do is to lend you my bicycle to help you get round the libraries quicker.'

'Oh, anything,' said the Professor, and taking the Colonel's bicycle, one of the old penny-farthing affairs, with one very big wheel and one very little one, he climbed into the saddle and wobbled off up the road.

The Professor wasn't much good at riding bicycles, and he ran into three carts, seven lamp-posts, a pond, and several policemen before he got to the library at North Pagwell, which was next on the list.

And when he did get to the library he couldn't stop, and went whizzing straight inside, scattering all sorts of studious-looking people about all over the floor.

'I beg all your pardons, I'm sure,' he gasped politely. Then, taking the book from the Library Man, he wheeled the bicycle outside, climbed up a lamp-post to get into the saddle, and rode off, leaving the book on the path, and had to come back all the way from West Pagwell to fetch it.

-AND WENT WHIZZING STRAIGHT INSIDE,-

Things went on like this for days and days. The Professor was getting quite expert at riding a bicycle, and could even read bits out of the book as he went along if there was nothing in the way. And the Library Men got to know him quite well.

'What's going to be the end of all this, I don't know,' graoned the Professor, dropping wearily into his chair after a strenuous ride up from Pagwell Docks. 'One book can't last fourteen libraries for ever. Something's got to happen soon.'

It hapged the very next day. All the fourteen Library Men came to tea with the Professor just after he'd got back from Pagwell Town.

ALL THE FOURTEEN LIBRARY MEN CAME IN TO TEA.

'Oh, how d'ye do,' he said, shaking hands with as many of them at once as he could, and hoping they hadn't come to say they'd found out about his losing the books, but feeling dreadfully scared in case they had.

'Nice weather,' said the Library Man from South Pagwell.

'And such a lot of it,' said the Pagwell Gardens man.

Then in came Mrs Flittersnoop with the tea.

After tea they started talking about things, and it wasn't long before they got round to the subject of lobsters.

'I always say that lobsters make better fathers than mothers,' said the Upper Pagwell man.

'Nonsense,' said the Lower Pagwell man, 'quite the other way about.'

'Let's look it up,' said the Pagwell Docks man. 'The Professor's got a copy of *The Life and Likings of a Lobster*, haven't you, Professor?'

'Certainly,' said the Professor. 'I'll fetch it. It's upstairs.'

He went upstairs and climbed out of his bedroom window. He slid down the drainpipe, got on the Colonel's bicycle, and pedalled away to the library at Pagwell Town for all he was worth. The wheels flew over the ground, people flew out of the way, dust flew up all over the place, and the Professor's coat-tails flew out behind.

How the Professor pedalled! How he panted and gasped, and how he hoped the Library Men wouldn't think he was too long getting the book.

At last – Pagwell Town. The Professor swerved and missed a bus by half an inch. It was the only time he was glad to miss a bus. He fell off the bicycle, fell into the library, gasped for the book, snatched it, and was bicycling back almost before the Assistant Library Man had let go of the book.

Back up the drainpipe he crawled and came down trying to look quite calm, but with his breath going *puff, puff, puff*, inside him, like a steam engine.

All the Library Men were looking at the books on his shelves.

'Here's the book, Professor,' said one of them, holding up a green volume. 'You didn't leave it upstairs.'

'No, it's here,' said another, and another, and another, and all the Library Men held up green books. They were all the copies of *The Life and*

Likings of a Lobster that the Professor had lost.

Yes, they were on his own bookshelves all the time. You see, he couldn't find them because he'd put each one among a different class of books. One copy he put under 'Lobsters', another he put under 'Biographies', another under 'Deep Sea Fishing', and another under 'How Much Do You know?' Still another he had put under 'Folk Lore' and one under 'Natural History', and so on. And each time he'd looked for the book he'd looked on the wrong section of his bookshelves, and, not seeing it, hadn't bothered to look there again. It was all very careless and complicated, but you see how it happened.

But it was all right now, and the Library Men took their own books back with them, though they couldn't make out why the Professor wanted fourteen copies of the same book.

'He's very clever, I tell you,' said the Pagwell Central man as they left the Professor's house. 'He probably reads them all at once in different chapters.'

From *The Incredible Adventures of Professor Branestawm*

RED FOX STORY COLLECTIONS

Meet some completely cool characters
and wild and wicked terrors in these brilliant
bumper bind-ups. COOL SCHOOL STORIES and
MORE COOL SCHOOL STORIES contains stories
that tells it how life really is in school. Find out
who invented the fearful 'teacher eater' in
BRILLIANTLY BAD STORIES.

COOL SCHOOL STORIES
The Worst Kids in the World and
The Worst Kids in the World Best School Year Ever
by Barbara Robinson
Wasim in the Deep End by Chris Ashley
Follow that Bus! by Pat Hutchins
0 09 926585 0 £4.99

MORE COOL SCHOOL STORIES
Runners by Susan Gates
Graphicat by Marilyn Watts
The Present Takers by Aidan Chambers
0 09 940023 5 £4.99

BRILLIANTLY BAD STORIES
complied by Barbara Ireson
Selected stories compiled from
Naughty Stories,
Even Naughtier Stories
and Naughtiest Stories
0 09 940128 2 £4.99

RED FOX STORY COLLECTIONS

Do you enjoy getting into the spirit of things? Step into the supernatural with the assortment of unearthly tales in SPOOKY STORIES. Experience the weird and wonderful worlds discovered in FREAKY STORIES and marvel at the amazing stories collected in MAGICAL MYSTERY STORIES.

MAGICAL MYSTERY STORIES

The Conjuror's Game by Catherine Fisher
The Thirteenth Owl by Nick Warburton
Words of Stone by Kevin Henks
0 09 940262 9 £4.99

FREAKY STORIES

The Runton Werewolf by Richie Perry
Henry Hollis and the Dinosaur by Willis Hall
Tom's Amazing Machine by Gordon Snell
0 09 940174 6 £4.99

SPOOKY STORIES

Seven Strange and Ghostly
Tales by Brian Jacques
The Creepy Tale by
Pichie Perry
A Legacy of Ghosts by
Colin Dann
0 09 940184 3 £4.99

RED FOX STORY COLLECTIONS

This series of value-for-money paperbacks each comprise several of your favourite stories in a single volume! Whether you want to follow the action-packed adventures of Hal and Roger Hunt in THE ADVENTURE COLLECTION or discover the myths surrounding Arthur and his Knights of the Round Table in KING ARTHUR STORIES these bumper reads are full of epic adventures and magical mystery.

THE ADVENTURE COLLECTION
by Willard Price
Whale Adventure and African Adventure
0 09 926592 3   £4.99

BIGGLES STORY COLLECTION
by Captain W. E. Johns
Biggles in France
Biggles Defend the Desert
Biggles: Foreign Legionnaire
0 09 940154 1   £4.99

KING ARTHUR STORIES
by Rosemary Sutcliff
The Sword and the Circle
The Light Beyond the Forest
The Road to Camlann
0 09 940164 9   £4.99

RED FOX STORY COLLECTIONS

If you are looking for a little animal magic then these brilliant bind-ups bring you stories of every creature, great and small. There are the fantastic creatures that Doctor Dolittle lives and works with in DOCTOR DOLITTLE STORIES, the bold and brave animals described in ANIMAL STORIES and there are three memorable tales of horse riding and friendship in PONY STORIES.

DOCTOR DOLITTLE STORIES
by Hugh Lofting
Selected stories from the Doctor Dolittle Books
0 09 926593 1 £4.99

ANIMAL STORIES
The Winged Colt of Casa Mia by Betsy Byars
Stories from Firefly Island by Benedict Blathwayt
Farthing Wood, The Adventure Begins
by Colin Dann
0 09 926583 4 £4.99

PONY STORIES
A Summer of Horses by
Carol Fenner
Fly-by-Night by K. M. Peyton
Three to Ride by Christine
Pullein-Thompson
0 09 940003 0 £4.99